Daily Bible Verses

Christian message and thoughts for each day of the year

Gwen Keegan

This book is available from Amazon.com and other online stores.

Cover art photograph by Gwen Keegan.

Copyright © 2017 Gwen Keegan.

All rights reserved.

ISBN: 1979627215
ISBN-13: 978-1979627214

DEDICATION

To all God's children

INTRODUCTION

"To every thing there is a season, and a time to every purpose under the heaven" (Ecclesiastes 3:1, The Holy Bible, King James Version). Do you put off doing things that you want to do? "I'll just do this first," then "I'll just do that first." Then you don't get around to the thing you wanted to do in the first place? If you already have a routine in place for daily prayers and devotions, you know what a comfort and a help this can be. If you are newly starting out on developing a habit of daily devotion, just know that there is no right time or wrong time. Whatever time works for you is great. You may have to try out different times until you find a good fit.

Some like having daily prayers in the mornings to set a good mood for the day. Some like having family prayers and Bible discussion at dinner time when the whole family is together. Or just after dinner when everyone can relax. Others choose the end of the day just before bedtime, so they can wind down their hectic day and talk over their joys and concerns with the Lord.

There are many ways to use the book. You might have this book at your breakfast or dinner table and let the first person who finishes eating read the daily section out loud to the others. Then everyone can discuss their thoughts and issues. Think about the discussion questions and share each family member's thoughts. For yourself, you may want to read the section in the morning when you wake up and think over the questions during the day.

Look at your typical day and decide where you would most benefit from daily prayers and devotions. Then start including this regularly until it becomes a habit.

Turn to today's date and begin - you will be glad you did!

January 1

"Seek the Lord and his strength, seek his face continually" (1 Chronicles 16:11 King James Version). Is it important that we get that bigger house or better car? Not likely. It is important that we draw closer to God and that we help our fellow human beings where we can. A New Year's prayer: We give thanks to You, O Lord for this bright shiny new year before us. Help us to seek a closer relationship with You. Help us become better witnesses for You during this year. Lead us, guide us and protect us we pray. In Jesus' name. Amen. What are some things that are important to you? Is there something new or different that you want to do in this coming new year?

January 2

"But they that wait upon the Lord shall renew their strength; they shall mount up with wings as eagles; they shall run, and not be weary; and they shall walk, and not faint" (Isaiah 40:31). We often make resolutions for the new year to renew our spirits. Resolving to read a chapter per day of the Bible is a good one. As with any resolution, just remember that missing a day does not mean that you should give up. Just read two the next day, or just pick up with reading one a day if that is all you can manage. But don't give up! Reading God's Word is a good way to become closer to Him. What are some other New Year's resolutions that you want to make for your Christian living?

January 3

If you do not feel worthy of God's love, you are in good company. Even John the Baptist said, "There cometh one mightier than I after me, the latchet of whose shoes I am not worthy to stoop down and unloose" (Mark 1:7 in part). We receive God's love through His grace and mercy, not because we are worthy of it and not because we earn it. Don't allow your feelings to keep you from seeking a relationship with God. Jesus is the only perfect one. He knows we are not perfect. We need not wait until we do some certain task before we look for God's love. It is there for us all for the asking. Open your Bible, open your heart. Is there anything that you are worried about? Have you brought it to the Lord in prayer? Call on Him for help.

January 4

"Thou shalt love thy neighbor as thyself (Matthew 19:19 in part). And in John 13:34 Jesus says, "A new commandment I give unto you, That ye love one another; as I have loved you, that ye also love one another." Jesus tells us to love the people around us as we love ourselves. We would need few other laws if we all took this seriously and acted with love toward everyone. Do you treat the people around you with respect? Do you try to help where you see a need? Think about how you could do more in these areas. When this becomes second nature to us, our world will be a more pleasant place to live.

January 5

"Giving thanks always for all things unto God and the Father in the name of our Lord Jesus Christ" (Ephesians 5:20). My daily prayer begins: O Lord, thank You for this day. Thank You for allowing us to be part of it. Thank You for giving Your Son to live and die and live again for us. Thank You, Jesus, for dying for our sins and for living Your life as an example to us of how to live ours. I pray that You would help us to do a better job of living to Your example. Help us to **understand** better and **do** better. Amen. Reading the Bible, doing Bible study and prayer are all ways to a better understanding of what Jesus wants us to do in our lives. How do you show brotherly love in your daily actions with others? Is there anything you would like to do differently to show that you follow Jesus?

January 6

Of course, it isn't always easy being Christian. At times, we pray for answers and can't find them. We don't always understand God's plan for us. At these times, we trust our faith in God and keep lifting our concerns in prayer. Always ending with, "Thy will be done" and trusting in God. Faith, love, and trust even in the face of uncertainty. Train yourself to see the good in situations and appreciate the positive wherever it can be found. "Blessed is the man that trusteth in the Lord, and whose hope the Lord is" (Jeremiah 17:7). What things in your life are you having trouble understanding? Have you shared these problems in prayer?

January 7

"Deliver my soul, O Lord, from lying lips, and from a deceitful tongue" (Psalm 120:2). We need to stop and think before passing along gossip which may be hurtful to someone. First – is it even true? Second – why are we passing it along? If it is just to appear "in the know" then we should reconsider and not pass along gossip that may harm someone else's reputation. If it is information that someone else needs to know, then we should pass it along in order to help the other person. Be sure to examine your reasons and not pass along gossip that is untrue or harmful. Have you ever seen anyone hurt by gossip? What can you do to stop this from happening?

January 8

I love to crochet. When I see yarn, I see the potential for what it could be. Soft pastel yarn becomes a lovely baby blanket, or strong yarn in a bold color becomes a stunning sweater under the movements of the right size crochet hook. Each yarn has different potential. I wonder if God gives our infant souls the potential to be soft nurturers, strong teachers, bold leaders and more. Then it is up to us to discover the right "crochet hooks" (school, mentor, church leader, etc.) to help us develop our talents and become the "sweater" that we are meant to be. What talents or interests do you have? How can you develop and encourage these talents and use them to praise the Lord? "For we are his workmanship, created in Christ Jesus unto good works, which God hath before ordained that we should walk in them" (Ephesians 2:10).

January 9

I just finished reading the Bible (King James Version)! It took one and a half years to complete. I read one or two chapters per day, then read a daily devotional book. Normally I would do the readings right after work when I sat down to begin my evening at home. This became an ingrained habit and I rarely missed a day. At first it was just a goal I set for myself. It quickly became a pleasure and I looked forward to the reading. Now that I have finished, I believe I will just start over at the beginning. There truly is comfort in the Good Book. "Blessed are they that hear the word of God, and keep it" (Luke chapter 11:28 in part). Have you read the entire Bible? If not, start now. If you have read it before, start over and do it again. What is one of your favorite passages?

January 10

Proverbs 20:11 says, "Even a child is known by his doings, whether his work be pure, and whether it be right." Do your best when you are doing any work. There is an old saying -if a job is worth doing, it is worth doing well. Whether it be school work, a paid job, or a volunteer job, you will be known by your efforts. You will have a good feeling of a job well done when you give your best efforts. Can you think of a time when you really gave your all to a project? How did you feel when the project was complete?

January 11

Psalm 98:1 says, in part, "O sing unto the Lord a new song; for he hath done marvelous things" and verse 4, in part, "Make a joyful noise unto the Lord, all the earth." One of my favorite parts of a worship service is the music and singing. The hymns of joy put a smile on the faces of the people and lift the hearts of all who hear. The words of the hymns are like prayer and praise. If you are ever feeling "down" try humming or singing a hymn, such as "Joy to the World." Or turn on the radio to some Gospel music. It lifts your spirits! Try to sing one song today. Do you find music uplifting? What is your favorite hymn?

January 12

The Bible tells us that Jesus said, "For God so loved the world, that he gave his only begotten Son, that whosoever believeth in him should not perish, but have everlasting life" (John 3:16). This well-loved Bible verse is usually recognized instantly just by saying "John 3, 16." Jesus goes on to say that He was sent not to condemn the world, but rather to save the world. All we have to do is accept Jesus into our hearts and receive the love. Open your heart and receive His love! Have you memorized any Bible verses? Pick a Bible verse and memorize it. What is one of your favorites?

January 13

I had a preacher who used to end church services by saying, "Go in peace. And may the God of Peace go with you." Remember that Jesus is not just with you on Sunday morning in church. He is as close as a prayer and as near as your thoughts. Take Him with you during the rest of the week as well as on Sundays. "But the fruit of the Spirit is love, joy, peace, longsuffering, gentleness, goodness, faith, Meekness, temperance" (Galatians 5:22-23 in part). Do you speak to Jesus in prayer every day? Pick a time for your daily prayers and soon it will become a habit. What do you need to pray for today?

January 14

Luke 18:16 says, "But Jesus called them unto him, and said, Suffer little children to come unto me, and forbid them not: for of such is the kingdom of God." When I heard this verse as a child, it gave me great comfort to know that I was welcomed to Jesus' side and that He would listen to me. Children can often feel left out around adults who seem to have more important business to attend to. Jesus has time for all of us. Is there anyone around you that seems to feel left out? Can you think of anything to do to make that person feel included?

January 15

"Not by works of righteousness which we have done, but according to his mercy he saved us" (Titus 3:5 in part). You do not have to measure up to some standard before you look for God. Jesus already gave His life for us on the cross. We just need to accept Him. We don't get there by ourselves, but all we need to do is ask Jesus for His help and forgiveness. "For by grace are ye saved through faith; and that not of yourselves: it is the gift of God: Not of works, lest any man should boast" (Ephesians 2:8-9). What ways can you think of to thank Jesus for giving His life for us?

January 16

"And oppress not the widow, nor the fatherless, the stranger, nor the poor; and let none of you imagine evil against his brother in your heart" (Zechariah 7:10). Martin Luther King Jr. worked to obtain equality for all people. We are all God's children and Jesus has commanded us to love one another. So, in a perfect world, we would all get along with each other and there would be no need for wars, treating people poorly or hate crimes. But evil does exist in the world and we need to stamp it out with love wherever we run into it. Increasing the problem by returning evil for evil does not help. Love and kindness is the best way to guard against evil actions. Where in your life do you see evil trying to grow? How might you introduce kindness into the situation?

January 17

"The Lord is my shepherd; I shall not want" (Psalm 23:1). This says it all. Jesus is *all* we need and *what* we need. He will guide us (or shepherd us) in the way we should go if we ask for His help and follow His will for our lives. Though it may not be the easy way and we may have trouble hearing or understanding His will, it is worth the effort. The important thing is to keep trying, keep praying. What would you like help with in your life? Do you have problems that you need to take to the Lord in prayer? Ask Him to guide you.

January 18

In Numbers 6:24-26, God gives Moses this blessing to say to the children of Israel, "The Lord bless thee, and keep thee: The Lord make his face shine upon thee, and be gracious unto thee: The Lord lift up his countenance upon thee, and give thee peace." When I was growing up, our youth fellowship meetings would end with this blessing. It always gave me a sense of comfort and peace to take with me into the world. Who would you like to share this blessing with today? How might you do that? If they are not near enough to talk to, could you write to them?

January 19

My prayer for my family and loved ones is that they will all know and love and serve the Lord. Whatever else they do in their life, this is the important thing. People measure success in many different ways. The only way that truly matters is that you know God. The love of God gives us that peace that passes understanding. That is what I want for my loved ones, above all. "And the peace of God, which passeth all understanding, shall keep your hearts and minds through Christ Jesus" (Philippians 4:7). Do you pray for your family and lift them up to the Lord? Can people tell by your actions that you are Christian? Think about what actions show Christian love.

January 20

"But seek ye first the kingdom of God, and his righteousness; and all these things shall be added unto you" (Matthew 6:33). One day at a time. In Matthew 6:25-34, Jesus tells us not to worry about tomorrow but rather deal with today, seeking first the kingdom of God. Sometimes our troubles overwhelm us, and we feel there is no way to get through everything we need to deal with. Break down the chores to the day by day necessities and ask God for strength to do what needs to be done, and for help to know His will. Take each day as it comes with God by your side. What things do you need help with? Lift them up to the Lord.

January 21

"Lord, help me be a better servant unto Thee." I say this in my prayers when I don't really know what to say, but just know I need some help. I figure that if I am following God's will for my life, then I am going in the right direction. Even when we can't see where we are going, God can. If I am serving God, I am doing the right things. "For ye have need of patience, that, after ye have done the will of God, ye might receive the promise" (Hebrews 10:36). Is there anything on your mind that you haven't quite known what to do about? Take it to the Lord in prayer.

January 22

Can you list the 10 Commandments? I grew up in the church and always thought I could rattle off the commandments at will. But to my surprise, I found I had to look them up recently! Here they are, for reference:
In Exodus 20:1-17 and again in Deuteronomy 5:1-22, God gives us these commandments (paraphrased here):

1. Thou shalt have no other gods before me.

2. Thou shalt not make unto thee any graven image.

3. Thou shalt not take the name of the Lord thy God in vain.

4. Remember the Sabbath day to keep it holy.

5. Honor thy father and thy mother.

6. Thou shalt not kill.

7. Thou shalt not commit adultery.

8. Thou shalt not steal.

9. Thou shalt not bear false witness against thy neighbor.

10. Thou shalt not covet thy neighbor's house, nor wife, nor servant, nor anything that is thy neighbor's.

A scribe asked Jesus which is the first commandment of all, "And Jesus answered him. The first of all the commandments is, Hear, O Israel; The Lord our God is one Lord: And thou shalt love the Lord thy God with all thy heart, and with all thy soul, and with all thy mind, and with all thy strength: this is the first commandment. And the second is like, namely this, Thou shalt love thy neighbor as thyself. There is none other commandment greater than these" (Mark 12:29-31).

And in the Gospel according to John 13:34, Jesus says, "A new commandment I give unto you, That ye love one another; as I have loved you, that ye also love one another." When you are wondering what to do in any situation, run through the commandments and you may find the answer. Do your daily actions follow the commandments?

January 23

"He that followeth after righteousness and mercy findeth life, righteousness, and honour" (Proverbs 21:21). Seek to do that which is right. Seems very simple but often is hard to do. What are some difficult decisions that you need to make? Have you lifted your concerns in prayer? Always remember to say, "Thy will be done" in your prayers. Talking things over with your church pastor may help also.

January 24

"Judge not, that ye be not judged" (Matthew 7:1). No one knows what another person is going through at any given time. It is better to be a friend, help, and offer understanding than to judge, condemn, and turn away. What situations have you run into where you would need understanding for yourself? Have you given the benefit of the doubt to someone in the past? A leap to judgement without all the facts often leads to regret. Hold off on judgement and take the time to understand.

January 25

"My little children, let us not love in word, neither in tongue; but in deed and in truth" (1 John 3:18). Actions speak louder than words. Show by your actions that you live a Christian life and you will be a daily witness for Jesus. By following the 10 commandments and the additional commandment to love one another, you may draw others to the Lord also. You never know who may be affected by your actions, so make a difference every day by example. Treat others as you would want to be treated yourself. Kindness shows! Can you think of anyone who needs a little extra kindness right now? How might you help them?

January 26

"And he arose, and rebuked the wind, and said unto the sea, Peace, be still. And the wind ceased, and there was great calm" (Mark 4:39). Jesus can command the earth, the sky and the seas. He could just force us all to behave properly but that is not what God desires. He gave us free will. Which means that we need to choose how to behave ourselves. It is more meaningful when we obey God's will purposefully by our conscious choice. Being human, we may still miss the mark at times, but if we ask forgiveness and try hard to behave better, God forgives us. Are there any areas in your life where you wish you would behave better? What could you do to make this happen?

January 27

"For ye are all the children of God by faith in Christ Jesus" (Galatians 3:26). When you run into someone who is different from you, many people tend to shy away from them or to treat them with suspicion. Other people are very curious and outgoing by nature and will want to approach the new person to learn all about them. Whatever your natural reaction is, remember that different doesn't mean bad. When you get to know someone, and understand their different background, you may feel more comfortable around them. Remember also that Jesus asks us to love our neighbor as ourselves. So, for His sake, let's make the effort to get to know and understand each other when we run into different cultures. Are there any people around you who are different from you and your family? How are they different? How are they similar?

January 28

"I have called upon thee, for thou wilt hear me, O God: incline thine ear unto me, and hear my speech" (Psalm 17:6). Sometimes the hard part of following Jesus is knowing where he wants us to go. Reading His Word in the Bible and praying for Him to guide us helps us to know what Jesus wants us to do. Ask yourself how you would explain your choices to Jesus if you could have a face to face talk with Him and see if the situation becomes clearer. After all, isn't prayer a form of face to face talks? What choices do you face? Have you talked them over with Him?

January 29

"I will lift up mine eyes unto the hills, from whence cometh my help. My help cometh from the Lord, which made heaven and earth" (Psalm 121:1-2). When you don't know which way to turn - turn to the Lord. Lift your concerns in prayer and receive God's help and comfort. Having made the heaven and earth, God can certainly help you with your problems. Trust in Him. What concerns do you have today? Take them to the Lord in prayer.

January 30

"Blessed are the merciful: for they shall obtain mercy" (Matthew 5:7). Have you ever been in a position where you can choose to either be kind to someone or to withhold your kindness and let them "get what they deserve"? For example, say Joe made an unflattering comment about you which you overheard. You aren't feeling very good towards Joe. Then Linda says to the group that she heard Joe had cheated on a test. You were there and know that he did not. You can either speak up and correct the impression or keep silent and let Joe's reputation suffer. What would Jesus do? Speak up and show mercy to Joe. You will feel better about yourself for doing so. Let your act of Christian mercy be a living example of the love of Christ. How do you show in your daily life that you follow Jesus?

January 31

Matthew chapter 5 verses 38 through 42 talks about turning the other cheek. The example from yesterday's reading may be thought of as both merciful and as turning the other cheek. Essentially Joe "slapped" you with his unkind comment and you turned the other cheek by not slapping him back, but rather doing him a kindness instead. In this way, your life shows by example what being a Christian means. People around you will see your Christian attitude and be drawn to Christ themselves. This is an excellent way to witness for the Lord. "Give to him that asketh thee, and from him that would borrow of thee turn not thou away" (Matthew 5:42). What are some other ways that a Christian attitude shows in day to day activities?

February 1

"And straightaway the father of the child cried out, and said with tears, Lord, I believe; help thou mine unbelief" (Mark 9:24). I often feel confused about conflicting beliefs. I know that God answers prayer – I have seen it happen. I also know that sometimes in my life it has seemed to me that my prayers were not answered. This is a time when I pray for God to help my unbelief and strengthen my faith. Humans are not all-knowing and sometimes have to realize that what we want may not be within God's plan for our lives – whether it makes sense to us or not. We are like small children who cry when their parents make them go to bed but they want to stay awake. They don't understand why their parents are being so mean. They are angry that Mom and Dad can't see that they want to stay up and play. The child does not understand that the parents know they are getting overtired and need sleep. When I don't get my way with God and it clearly seems (to me!) that I should – I think of this example and take it on faith that God's plan for me is better than any plan I could come up with on my own. What have you ever felt that God did not answer your prayers about? Looking back, does it still seem that way to you?

February 2

"Let us therefore follow after the things which make for peace, and things wherewith one may edify another" (Romans 14:19). A prayer: Lord, help us to do Thy will and forgive us our sins. Help us to help each other and learn from each other. Help us get along better and stop the hate and the hate crimes in the world. Help us learn to love one another as You have commanded. Amen. We will need to get to know and understand others in order to have peace. Unfounded prejudice can get in the way of understanding and interacting with others in a positive way. Have you ever felt as though you did not like someone before you actually met them? Were you able to put that feeling aside and give the new person a chance?

February 3

"For all have sinned, and come short of the glory of God" (Romans 3:23). Don't think that because you do not feel that you have earned a place beside Jesus that you should stay away from church or avoid prayer. In truth, it is not possible to *earn* our place with Jesus - it is only through God's grace and mercy that we are received. This grace and mercy is available to even the worst sinner you can imagine. Believe and accept God's love. Do you have any worries about Jesus accepting you? Lay your worries at His feet through prayer.

February 4

"And they that know thy name will put their trust in thee: for thou, Lord, hast not forsaken them that seek thee" (Psalm 9:10). Airplane rides scare me. I probably say more prayers on the days I fly than any other days. It occurred to me at some point that I was pestering God with my repeated requests for a safe trip. When I find myself doing this, I have started apologizing for not trusting the Lord to hear me the first time. I ask instead for God to calm my fears, strengthen my faith, and for His will to be done. My stress level sinks when I put myself in the hands of the Lord. What fears do you have? Do you share them with the Lord and accept His comfort?

February 5

"A soft answer turneth away wrath: but grievous words stir up anger" (Proverbs 15:1). Sometimes we say hurtful things when we are angry. It is important not to blurt out things that we don't even mean. Once said aloud, there is no way to "un-say" them no matter how much you may wish you could. Take a minute to mentally bite your tongue and think over what you are going to say before you say something you will regret. While it is also important to express your feelings, there are often more reasonable ways to say something. Have you ever said something without thinking, then wished you had not spoken? How might things have been different if you had waited until you thought about your words?

February 6

"Blessed be God, even the Father of our Lord Jesus Christ, the Father of mercies, and the God of all comfort" (2 Corinthians 1:3). Sadness affects many people at one time or another. For some it happens by the seasons of the year and for others it comes at any time of the year. Recognizing that you are feeling sadness or depression sometimes helps to counteract its effects. If you are sad, think about the reasons you may be depressed or sad and take each one to God in prayer. Then think of all the reasons you have to be happy and share those in prayer as well. Receive His comfort. Do you notice anyone around you who seems sad and may need to talk to someone? What might you do to help?

February 7

"If we say that we have no sin, we deceive ourselves, and the truth is not in us. If we confess our sins, he is faithful and just to forgive us our sins, and to cleanse us from all unrighteousness" (1 John 1:8-9). Becoming Christian does not mean that you will never sin again. I have found myself coveting something that is my neighbor's. But I don't act upon it. I try to get past it and I ask for forgiveness. We are not perfect. We often need to confess, repent of our sins (be sorry for our sins), and ask for forgiveness. The good news is that Jesus does hear and forgive us. The more we read God's Word and try to live to Jesus' example, the more able we are to follow God's will. What thoughts or actions do you need Jesus' help in correcting? Talk it over with Him.

February 8

When I feel that I am being pulled by the world to behave in ways I know in my heart to be wrong, I remember what the Bible says in Luke 4:7-8. Satan said to Jesus, "If thou therefore wilt worship me, all shall be thine. And Jesus answered and said unto him, Get thee behind me, Satan: for it is written, Thou shalt worship the Lord thy God, and him only shalt thou serve." I read these words aloud and feel the strength to behave in the way Jesus would want me to, and not in the way other people are pulling me. It could be pressure to use drugs, or pressure to treat someone else poorly, or even just pressure to buy things I know I can't afford. What are some pressures you feel that you know in your heart are wrong? Think about how you will handle these situations in a manner pleasing to God.

February 9

"In all things shewing thyself a pattern of good works: in doctrine shewing uncorruptness, gravity, sincerity" (Titus 2:7). How do you show that you are Christian in your daily life? One of the most important ways is to treat other people as you would want them to treat you. And to do so in Jesus' name and for His sake. People notice how you treat others more than you might think. Your actions may draw others to Jesus without you even being aware of it. What other ways might you show that you follow Jesus?

February 10

In Mark 2:16-17 the church leaders asked the disciples about why Jesus would eat and drink with sinners. Jesus answered, "I came not to call the righteous, but sinners to repentance" (Mark 2:17 in part). Jesus walked among those people who needed to hear His message. He did not close himself off from the sinners. Today we can follow His example and talk to people who need to hear His message wherever we find them. While it is uplifting to keep company with other Christians, we need to remember to widen our circles to include others and be a witness for God through our actions as well as our words. What are some ways that you might reach out to other people?

February 11

"And Jesus said unto them, I am the bread of life: he that cometh to me shall never hunger; and he that believeth on me shall never thirst" (John 6:35). Faith sustains and nourishes or feeds us. Our walk with Jesus feeds our soul and gives us peace. In today's hectic world we need our time in prayer and devotion to renew our spirit. Have you made time for daily prayers? If not, figure out a time that works best for you and begin. Do you remember to take Jesus with you throughout the day?

February 12

"I will praise thee, O Lord, with my whole heart; I will shew forth all thy marvelous works" (Psalm 9:1). The beauty of a sunrise, the budding of new flowers in the spring, any of the wonderful sights that God created can fill our hearts with joy. Let us remember to give thanks for all the splendors we see. What brings a smile to your face and a grateful prayer to your mind? Give thanks for all beauty around you this day.

February 13

"Now the God of hope fill you with all joy and peace in believing, that ye may abound in hope, through the power of the Holy Ghost" (Romans 15:13). When you know the love of God you want others to also know that love. Sharing the Word and passing along God's peace becomes important to you. Where and how might you share God's love in your everyday life? Think of ways to begin to do so.

February 14

"If any man serve me, let him follow me; and where I am, there shall also my servant be: if any man serve me, him will my Father honour" (John 12-26).
Thank you, Jesus
For Your love
For grace and mercy
From above.
Thank You for each blessing
That You have sent my way.
Help me be Your servant
Through each and every day. Amen.

What blessings has God given you? Have you remembered to say, "thank You" in prayer?

February 15

"Pride goeth before destruction, and an haughty spirit before a fall" (Proverbs 16:18). The type of pride that leads to destruction is the selfish, gloating pride that raises the self over the Lord who gave you the strengths, talents, or intelligence to make the effort that is the source of pride. It is normal to be pleased with our efforts, but not to the point of raising yourself over others. When humbleness replaces pride and when credit is given to God, you will find more joy in your accomplishments. What are some things that you have done that you are proud of? What strengths or talents did God bless you with that made you able to do so well?

February 16

"I will sing unto the Lord as long as I live: I will sing praise to my God while I have my being" (Psalm 104:33). I praise God for the healing I have seen Him do in my family. Praise Him for leading me to the relationships I have needed. Praise Him for leading me away from bad situations. Praise Him for His love and comfort in my life. What would you praise God for today? Say a prayer of thankfulness for these things.

February 17

"For where envying and strife is, there is confusion and every evil work. But the wisdom that is from above is first pure, then peaceable, gentle, and easy to be entreated, full of mercy and good fruits, without partiality, and without hypocrisy" (James 3:16-17). Being hypocritical (saying one thing and doing something different) is one of the things that I battle against. I want to do my part to show the love of Christ through my daily living. However, I sometimes catch myself being unkind, such as making an unfair remark about someone. Often jealousy or envy is involved at the root of my feelings. When I catch myself about to put someone down I try to stop before those unkind words come out of my mouth. I say that I love my neighbor as myself, so it is hypocritical to say unkind things about them. Instead I channel my thoughts to all the blessings I have to be thankful for and I ask God to help me let go of jealousy, envy or negative thoughts. What things or actions do you struggle against and need God's help? Take these things to Him in prayer.

February 18

"Be not overcome of evil, but overcome evil with good" (Romans 12:21). It is hard not to be overwhelmed with the evil we find in the world, but the Bible tells us to overcome the evil with good. Sometimes we can step in ourselves and sometimes, especially if you are a child, we need to call for help with a situation. For example, if you see someone being bullied and can safely step in to help that person – you are overcoming evil with good. However, if the situation is dangerous, calling 911 may be necessary rather than stepping in by yourself. What are some situations you can think of to offer up good to overcome evil? How might you go about that safely?

February 19

"O give thanks unto the Lord; for he is good; for his mercy endureth for ever" (1 Chronicles 16:34). Look around and see what blessings are in your life. Think of the good things that fill your heart with love. Think of the supports and encouragements that you receive. Give thanks for the good in your life. And if negative thoughts surface – think of how to overcome these problems in life, with God's help to guide you. What do you need God's help with today? What blessings do you have in your life?

February 20

"O come, let us sing unto the Lord: let us make a joyful noise to the rock of our salvation. Let us come before his presence with thanksgiving, and make a joyful noise unto him with psalms" (Psalm 95:1-2). Nothing lifts my spirits up more than music or song. You don't even have to be good at it to enjoy it! Try singing hymns in the shower or playing gospel music while you work around the house. It enriches the soul. What is your favorite church song? Sing it out loud today.

February 21

"Keep thy tongue from evil, and thy lips from speaking guile. Depart from evil, and do good; seek peace, and pursue it" (Psalm 34:13-14). This sums up our wishes for getting through each day. Staying away from evil and doing some good where we can. Seeking peace is a worthy goal and prayer can help us get there. Acting on evil thoughts is not the Christian way. Have you ever been the one to "keep the peace" by talking those around you into calming down? How might things have turned out differently had you not stepped in?

February 22

"O give thanks unto the Lord; call upon his name: make known his deeds among the people" (Psalm 105:1). God wants us to talk to Him and to spread His Word to all people. There are many ways to minister and witness for the Lord. Different people have different talents and interests. Some serve by singing in the choir, some by helping at homeless shelters, some by speaking at events, some by reading to shut-ins or nursing home residents and many other ways. What other ways can you think of? What ways fit in with your particular interests?

February 23

"Have mercy upon me, O God, according to thy lovingkindness: according unto the multitude of thy tender mercies blot out my transgressions" (Psalm 51:1). This was written so long ago and yet still applies easily to us today. We are blessed indeed that God chooses to show us grace and mercy. Praise the Lord. What blessings do you count in your life? Give thanks for each one.

February 24

"Ponder the path of thy feet, and let all thy ways be established" (Proverbs 4:26). Proverbs advises us to think about where we are heading and how we are getting there. Talk your plans over with God through prayer and be sure you are following His will for your life, in a manner pleasing to Him. Set out your goals with clearly thought out plans to achieve those goals. But we must also be ready to change our plans if God leads us in another direction. In what direction is your life headed?

February 25

"Train up a child in the way he should go: and when he is old, he will not depart from it" (Proverbs 22:6). It does take a village to raise a child. We should all pitch in to help children learn and grow. There are many different ways to help. Invite some neighbor kids to go to vacation bible school? Pitch in and help teach Sunday school class? What other ways can you think of that will help children to know the Lord?

February 26

Joy can fill us with happy feelings and make us want to share those feelings with others. Remember to share your joys with Jesus in prayer. You don't want to seek God only in times of trouble – seek Him in times of joy also and your joy will be increased. "Rejoice in the Lord alway: and again I say, Rejoice" (Philippians 4:4). What happiness would you share with the Lord today? Take it to Him in prayer.

February 27

Bullies are often unhappy people who feel the need to put someone down in order to feel better about themselves. They are not following the commandment to love one another and may need to be reminded that we are all God's children. They may not feel God's love themselves. In Matthew 18:20 Jesus says, "For where two or three are gathered together in my name, there am I in the midst of them." Let your interactions with others show by example that you follow Jesus' teachings. If you are being bullied yourself, how might you respond in a way that does not buy into the bully's taunts? And a way that shows that you are confident in the love of God? Share the love of God and a bully may become a friend.

February 28

"My son, if sinners entice thee, consent thou not" (Proverbs 1:10). This sounds so simple, but can be very hard. Peer pressure is often very strong, even when we know we do not want to follow along. Practicing ways to say, "No" beforehand can be helpful. Having a ready answer of, "that's not for me" or simply, "no, thanks" can help you remove yourself from risky situations. What peer pressures are facing you? How will you handle them? Practice some responses.

February 29

"Recompense to no man evil for evil. Provide things honest in the sight of all men" (Romans 12:17). Think over your actions before you take that action. Is it the right thing to do? Is it something you will end up regretting? A moment's pause can save you a long regret. Prayer can keep you grounded and healthy. Are you facing any decisions that you have doubts about? Lift your concerns in prayer.

March 1

"...and I will cause the shower to come down in his season; there shall be showers of blessings" (Ezekiel 34:26 in part).
Rain is falling all around
Quickly soaking in the ground
So many raindrops, I can't count
Like the many blessings, in large amount.
Blessings from the Lord above
Each one sent with God's own love.
We thank You, Lord, for every one.
Especially for the gift of Your own Son.
Thank You for each blessed day
In Jesus' Holy Name we pray. Amen.

What blessings are you thankful for today?

March 2

The season of Lent begins each year on a different date, but falls in late February or early March. Lent is a time of repentance and reflection prior to Easter. Ash Wednesday marks the beginning of Lent. The mark of ashes on the forehead signifies that we came from dust. "...for dust thou art, and unto dust thou shalt return"

(Genesis 3:19 in part) and that we need to repent our sins to be redeemed. Typically, people give up something during the 40 days of Lent, just as Jesus fasted for 40 days in the desert. Prayer, fasting and giving to others is the hallmark of Lent. Many people give up a certain food during Lent. This would be a good time to give up grudges against other people or give up petty jealousies as well. Practice forgiveness. What things do you need to give up and let go of? Start by asking Jesus to help you.

March 3

"I have shewed you all things, how that so laboring ye ought to support the weak, and to remember the words of the Lord Jesus, how he said, It is more blessed to give than to receive" (Acts 20:35). Living a Christian life should include helping others in whatever ways you can. Helping to feed the hungry by donating your time and/or food to a food bank is one way to help. Bolstering other people around you when you hear a need in someone's voice is another. Offering a listening ear to a friend with a problem is another. Simple common courtesies done in Jesus' name can make all the difference in someone's life when they most need support. What other ways can you think of to help others?

March 4

"Let all bitterness, and wrath, and anger, and clamour, and evil speaking, be put away from you, with all malice: And be ye kind one to another, tenderhearted, forgiving one another, even as God for Christ's sake hath forgiven you" (Ephesians 4:31-32). Do not keep negative feelings in your heart as you will harm yourself by holding on to those feelings. Explore it, understand it, then forgive and put it behind you. Are you holding on to feelings that are not good for you? Talk it over with God. Begin the process of letting go and keep praying until you are able to let go.

March 5

"For if they fall, the one will lift up his fellow: but woe to him that is alone when he falleth; for he hath not another to help him up"

(Ecclesiastes 4:10). Where and how do children learn kindness, respect and love? Hopefully it starts at home and continues in their community, school and church. Church can be an important resource for any family and particularly for single parent families. Adults going it alone need all the help and support they can find. If this is your situation, try sharing your life with a church family. You may find some help for yourself and some support for caring for your family within the congregation. If you are part of a church congregation, pay special attention to anyone who may need your help. The old saying "to have a friend – be a friend" comes to mind. Jesus wants us to help each other. Who do you think of that might need your help? How might you be able to help them?

March 6

"Let the words of my mouth, and the meditation of my heart, be acceptable in thy sight, O Lord, my strength, and my redeemer" (Psalm 19:14). These are words to live up to on a daily basis. Let us always think before we speak and be sure Jesus would approve of our thoughts and actions. And let us always remember that Jesus is our strength and our redeemer. Our words and deeds are our witness to Jesus' role in our lives. Would someone, who did not know you, be able to tell that you are Christian? How might you show that you follow Jesus?

March 7

"And we have known and believed the love that God hath to us. God is love; and he that dwelleth in love dwelleth in God, and God in him" (1 John 4:16).
(A rap song –)
I'm a child of God – that is me
About God's love is what I be.
I want you to know Him too
Feel God's love, through and through.
Jesus died for you and me
From our sins to set us free.
Now our job is to love each other
Treat each one as a sister or a brother.

Straight up love from the heart
Come on people do your part.
What I'm sayin' through this patter
We're all God's children, all lives matter!
Prayer and praise to God above
Open your heart, feel His Love.
Pass along His peace, always be kind
Help each other out, when someone's in a bind.
Spread the joy, spread His Word
Lift your voice and be heard.
Share God's love everywhere you can.
God bless you! Hallelujah! Amen.

How do you treat other people? Does kindness show in your actions?

March 8

"But without faith it is impossible to please him; for he that cometh to God must believe that he is, and that he is a rewarder of them that diligently seek him" (Hebrews 11:6). When and where do you say your daily prayers? If you do not already have a habit of daily prayers, there is no time like the present to pick one. At the start of the day when you first wake up, before you even get out of bed is a good time for some. At the end of the day when you sit down to rest, or as you head for bed may suit you. Choose a time that suits your life style and can become a daily habit. Grow in your faith. Carefully seek Him.

March 9

"I can do all things through Christ which strengtheneth me" (Philippians 4:13). This is a very powerful verse and very reassuring. Christ will give us strength to cope with our daily lives if we ask Him for help. We can lean on Him and know that we are not alone and not on our own. What things do you need help with, or need to bring to God in prayer? Ask for Jesus to help you and receive strength from Him.

March 10

"This is the day which the Lord has made; we will rejoice and be glad in it" (Psalm 118:24). What a nice way to begin the day. Remembering that each day is a gift from God and is a reason to be thankful. What are some other things that you are thankful for? Family may be top on your list. Good health, friends, and a joyful heart are some others. If you don't have those things that you wish for now, ask God to guide you on a path to getting the best health you can have, or the friends and family that you want to have. Always remembering to end with, "Thy will be done, not mine" as God may have other plans that are not clear to you yet.

March 11

"Let your light so shine before men, that they may see your good works, and glorify your Father which is in heaven" (Matthew 5:16). What talents has God given to you? Are you developing those talents to use for His praise and glory? We all have different abilities and interests. Use yours to witness for God, giving the glory to Him.

March 12

"Therefore, my beloved brethren, be ye stedfast, unmoveable, always abounding in the work of the Lord, forasmuch as ye know that your labour is not in vain in the Lord" (1 Corinthians 15:58). Doing God's work involves helping wherever we see the need and using what resources we have (not just money but also time, effort, talents, support, etc.). Work within our church and in our community as well as in the global community. Jesus died for us all, not just for a certain few. Even though we may not look alike or act alike, we are all God's children and need to work together. What ways can you think of to help others in need?

March 13

"And this is the will of him that sent me, that every one which seeth the Son, and believeth on him, may have everlasting life: and

I will raise him up at the last day" (John 6:40). A prayer: Lord help us through this day. Help us to know Your will for our lives and give us the strength to follow Your will. Surround our family and loved ones with Your love and protection. Help us to recognize our sins, to ask for forgiveness, and to turn away from sin. Help us to help each other. In Jesus' name. Amen. Can you think of a time when you thought about doing something, but realized it was wrong, so did not do it? Jesus gives us strength to turn away from wrong-doing when we ask Him.

March 14

"I will bless the Lord at all times: his praise shall continually be in my mouth. My soul shall make her boast in the Lord: the humble shall hear thereof, and be glad" (Psalm 34:1-2). All through our day we can keep God near our hearts and minds. Be quick to give Him the praise for blessings received. And be quick to give thanks on joyful occasions. Praise the Lord! What in your life brings you joy? Give thanks for these joys in prayer.

March 15

"The Lord is nigh unto all them who call upon him, to all that call upon him in truth" (Psalm 145:18). God is always near to us, even when we feel most alone. Talk to Him through prayer and pour out your feelings to Him. His healing presence can make even the worst problems become manageable. Are you facing problems where you need His help? If so, talk to Him. If not – give thanks!

March 16

"If any of you lack wisdom, let him ask of God, that giveth to all men liberally, and upbraideth not; and it shall be given him" (James 1:5). Just as our cell phones need to plug in to get recharged, so do our spiritual lives need recharging. Plug in to the power of prayer and talk to Jesus. Ask whatever you need to know. Share your burdens as well as your joys. Be thankful and humble and receive your fresh charge from the Lord. Then you can meet the day with a renewed spirit and loving attitude. Is your attitude in need of recharging? Ask for His help.

March 17

"Finally, my brethren, be strong in the Lord, and in the power of his might. Put on the whole armour of God, that ye may be able to stand against the wiles of the devil" (Ephesians 6:10-11). My aim in life is to be seen as a Christian by my actions. I want to witness for the Lord in such a way that people know why I am joyous, forgiving, helpful, humble and many other things without my just telling them (although I do that too when the opportunity presents). If my being Christian doesn't show, then I am doing something wrong. Or not doing something right. The focus should be on Jesus – praise for Him, not on myself. Actions speak louder than words and I want to live out loud for Jesus. What might you praise the Lord for giving you? How do your actions show this?

March 18

"And now abideth faith, hope, charity, these three; but the greatest of these is charity" (1 Corinthians 13:13). Goodwill towards our fellow citizens is a hallmark of Christian living. It can take many forms, one of which is helping those less fortunate than yourself. You can give of your money, time, talents, or a combination of these. If you have the money to spare you might donate money to a foodbank. Or you might donate your time by helping to serve at a homeless shelter. You might use your talents to help a shelter organize a food drive. There are many different ways to help out. What other ways can you think of to help?

March 19

Flowers and food crops all need the rain, good soil and sunshine in order to grow and be healthy. Our spiritual lives also need nourishment in order to thrive. Jesus said, "But whosoever drinketh of the water that I shall give him shall never thirst; but the water that I shall give him shall be in him a well of water springing up into everlasting life" (John 4:14). Feed your soul with the Word of God, with communication through prayer, and companionship of fellow Christians. How do you feed your Christian faith?

March 20

Words to live by. "And be ye kind one to another, tenderhearted, forgiving one another, even as God for Christ's sake hath forgiven you" (Ephesians 4:32). How do you behave in your everyday life that fits in with this passage? Are you able to let go of negative feelings and work out differences with others? If you have problems, talk them over with God. If you need to forgive someone, do it now, with God's help. You will feel better for letting go of anger or hurt feelings.

March 21

The human race (sometimes referred to as a rat race!) is not a sprint race. It is a long endurance race, so slow and steady wins the race. And we can all win – there is not just one winner. The finish line is heaven and the journey is as important as the ending. To prepare for the race, study the Bible, learn Jesus' teachings and live by those teachings. Remember that the Human Race includes us all, so run the good race by helping each other wherever you can. We do not *earn* our place in Heaven, we will get there only through God's grace and mercy. "But unto every one of us is given grace according to the measure of the gift of Christ" (Ephesians 4:7). How do you make sure that you are running a good race?

March 22

The date for celebrating Easter changes every year. It falls in late March or April. As a child growing up in the church, I took this for granted. It made no difference to me which date was used. When I became curious as to why the date varies, I did some research and found a complicated explanation that involved the differences in solar and lunar calendars, full moon occurrences and when the Passover occurs. A computer search yields multiple articles on the subject if you are interested in further detail. The important thing is to celebrate the Resurrection, not on which day we celebrate.

Truly, we should celebrate every day the important news that Jesus lives! "And he saith unto them, Be not affrighted: Ye seek Jesus of Nazareth, which was crucified: he is risen; he is not here" (Mark 16:6 in part). Hallelujah! Do you carry the good news that Jesus lives within your heart? Celebrate!

March 23

Easter is a time of renewal. The winter is over, and spring is showing us new growth. The world feels fresh and new. It is the perfect time to celebrate the risen Lord. And the perfect time to renew our faith. That God loves us so much He gave His Son and that Jesus loves us enough to die for us is truly a miracle. We are asked to believe and to love one another. Go into the world and do your part! "Jesus said unto her, I am the resurrection, and the life: he that believeth in me, though he were dead, yet shall he live" (John 11:25). Can you think of anyone who needs to hear this good news? What might you do to share it with them?

March 24

"And he took bread, and gave thanks, and brake it, and gave unto them, saying, This is my body which is given for you: this do in remembrance of me. Likewise also the cup after supper, saying, This cup is the new testament in my blood, which is shed for you" (Luke 22:19-20). Maundy Thursday is the Thursday before Easter when Jesus had The Last Supper with His disciples. Maundy is derived from the Latin word for command. Jesus washed the feet of His disciples and commanded them to love one another. Would you treat others differently if you saw them as Jesus sees them? Think about what it would mean to love one another first and then to try to solve our differences. It is easier to come to agreements with others when we have respect for them as a person.

March 25

"And Jesus answered them, saying, The hour is come, that the Son of man should be glorified" (John 12:23). Little children may think of jelly beans, Easter bunnies, candy and Easter egg hunts when they think of Easter time. We need to see that they understand that those things are just for fun and are not the main event. Jesus is the reason for the season. What can you do to make sure the children in your life know that Jesus loves them? Take a child to church; witness for the Lord by the way you live your life; see that they have children's Bibles to read. What else can you think of to help?

March 26

"And they found the stone rolled away from the sepulcher. And they entered in, and found not the body of the Lord Jesus" (Luke 24:2-3). "Christ is risen!" "He is risen indeed!" This is a lovely Easter greeting. It may have started thousands of years ago, but the joy is still new to us today, and the miracle is still full of wonder. Jesus died so that our sins could be forgiven through the grace and mercy of God. Have you said, "Thank You, Lord" lately? Take a moment in prayer to say, "Thank You" for this greatest of gifts.

March 27

In 1 Thessalonians 5:17, the Bible tell us to "Pray without ceasing." I made a habit for myself of saying my daily prayers in the morning. I also say smaller prayers during the day as events occur that call for prayer. Such as a quick prayer right away upon finding out that someone I know is sick, or a quick prayer for help when the news tells of a disaster. Sometimes just saying what is on your mind comes more easily than trying to compose the perfect prayer. I believe that being in constant readiness to pray keeps us closer to God. What kind of things bring you to prayer?

March 28

"Be still, and know that I am God" (Psalm 46:10 in part). When I find myself becoming frantic for an answer to a problem, or for some action to take place that is beyond my control, I find comfort in this verse. I am reminded to "let go and let God." While I may want immediate actions, that may not be in God's plan for me. As Psalm 37:7 says (in part), "Rest in the Lord, and wait patiently for him." I need to call upon my faith, calm down, and listen for God's will for my life. What situations cause you to be impatient with answers to prayer? Once you realize that you are rushing things, do you relax and trust in the Lord?

March 29

"Cast thy burden upon the Lord, and he shall sustain thee" (Psalm 55:22 in part). Share your problems with the Lord in prayer and ask for wisdom to deal with them in a way that pleases God. Even when you can't find words, just saying, "Lord, I lift this up to Thee - help me to do Thy will" gets you started. God knows what is in your heart and what is going on even when you have trouble expressing yourself. Are there things in your life that you have trouble putting into words? Lift them up in silent prayer.

March 30

"Then was Jesus led up of the Spirit into the wilderness to be tempted of the devil" (Matthew 4:1). Temptations are all around us. Matthew chapter 4 tells of the temptations Jesus experienced. What temptations do you face today? Drug use is a common temptation that most of us face at some point in our lives. Knowing the dangers of drugs before hand and practicing how to say, "No" in different situations can help give you the confidence to turn them down. At times even people who you think of as good friends may be the ones who tempt you with things that are bad for you. A simple, "No, thank you" may be hard to say, but may be the most important decision you can make. Call upon Jesus to help keep you strong in your decision. Your example may be affecting more people than you know. Have you ever had to say, "No" to a friend? How did you handle that?

March 31

"For in that he himself hath suffered being tempted, he is able to succor them that are tempted" (Hebrews 2:18). Another common temptation comes from peer pressure to partake in behavior that you are not comfortable with at the time. It could be bullying another person, engaging in behavior that makes you nervous, trying drugs, alcohol or tobacco, or many other things - any attempt to get you to behave in a way that makes you feel bad. Listen to your feelings and don't be convinced to follow the leader if you do not like where the behavior is taking you. Stop and take a minute to say to yourself, "Jesus help me." Then remove yourself from the situation. What things in your life are others trying to tempt you into doing? How will you respond?

April 1

"But let all those that put their trust in thee rejoice: let them ever shout for joy, because thou defendest them: let them also that love thy name be joyful in thee" (Psalm 5:11). Trust in the Lord and ask Him to guide you. We can rejoice that God is able and that He listens to us when we pray. The Bible tells us that a joyful heart is pleasing to God. What things are you thankful for? What brings joy to your heart? Share that in prayer.

April 2

"And let the beauty of the Lord our God be upon us: and establish thou the work of our hands upon us; yea, the work of our hands establish thou it" (Psalm 90:17). What different works do your hands do during a normal day? Would Jesus approve of your behaviors toward others? A prayer: Let me show in my everyday behavior that I follow Thee, Lord. Let the work of my hands be for Thee. Keep me ever mindful of how my actions can affect others. And let me always be a positive witness for Jesus. Amen.

April 3

If you find yourself feeling down in the dumps, just remember that Jesus loves you so much that he died for you. Bask in His love and renew your spirit. Whatever it is that has you feeling low – Jesus can help. Give it all to Him and pour out your feelings. Do you have any sadness in your life right now? Are there things that you need to lift up to Jesus in prayer? He understands what is in your heart even better than you do yourself. Let His healing love surround you. "But my God shall supply all your need according to his riches in glory by Christ Jesus" (Philippians 4:19).

April 4

Are you as considerate of your family members as you are of your everyday friends? Many times we treat strangers better than we treat our relatives simply because we feel like we don't have to be on our best behavior around family. Jesus tells us to love one another as He has loved us. Don't forget that this includes your family. Talk to each other, pray for each other, and support one another. "Be kindly affectioned one to another with brotherly love; in honour preferring one another" (Romans 12:10). Say a prayer for your family.

April 5

"A man's pride shall bring him low: but honour shall uphold the humble in spirit" (Proverbs 29:23). Feeling good about your accomplishments is a good thing - as long as we don't get over pride-full and full of ourselves. Remember to give God the credit. He gave you those talents to begin with. And letting others know where your strength comes from may help lead others to God as well. What talents do you want to develop? How can you use them to the glory of God?

April 6

"And why take ye thought for raiment? Consider the lilies of the field, how they grow; they toil not, neither do they spin. And yet I say unto you, That even Solomon in all his glory was not arrayed like one of these" (Matthew 6:28-29).
Flowers budding, blooming open
Trees in glorious color showing
Spring arrives with freshened air
Gentle breezes blowing.
Lord, You have given us such splendor
On display for all to see.

For this beautiful earth
Humbly, gratefully, we thank Thee. Amen.

What things are you thankful for this day? Let God know through prayer.

April 7

The Bible tells us to "Cease from anger, and forsake wrath: fret not thyself in any wise to do evil" (Psalm 37:8). Letting go of anger is a healing activity. The more tightly you hold on to anger, the more you yourself suffer – not the person with whom you are angry. Try to understand and forgive. Lift your concerns up to Jesus and give them to Him. Do you have anger toward anyone or anything that you need to let go of? Ask for Jesus' help through prayer.

April 8

"For thou art my rock and my fortress; therefore for thy name's sake lead me and guide me" (Psalm 31:3). Do you bring your problems to the Lord in prayer? Do you look first for His help before taking actions? We often forget to ask for help and then find ourselves in trouble. A prayer: Thank You, Lord, for all the blessings You have given us. Help us to know Your will for our lives, and give us the strength to follow Your will. You have given us free will and we freely seek to follow You. In Jesus' name. Amen.

April 9

Lift your problems or concerns to the Lord in prayer. "Blessed be the Lord, because he hath heard the voice of my supplications" (Psalm 28:6). What do you need help with today? Do you have decisions to make that have you unsure? Prayer and more prayer is the answer! Continue to ask for His strength for one day at a time. "The Lord is my rock, and my fortress, and my deliverer; my God, my strength, in whom I will trust" (Psalm 18:2 in part).

April 10

"The Lord is my strength and my shield; my heart trusted in him, and I am helped: therefore my heart greatly rejoiceth; and with my song will I praise him" (Psalm 28:7). Work hard, play hard, pray hard. This will exercise you physically, mentally and spiritually. Having a robust prayer life keeps you spiritually grounded in faith. What do you think of to praise the Lord for today? What do you need His help with right now?

April 11

"God is our refuge and strength, a very present help in trouble" (Psalm 46:1). A prayer: O Lord, be with all my loved ones. Help us with our needs of the moment, according to Your will for our lives. Help us to know what You would have us to do. And give us strength to follow Your will. Amen. What are your present needs? Have you asked the Lord for His help?

April 12

"Make a joyful noise unto the Lord, all ye lands. Serve the Lord with gladness: come before his presence with singing" (Psalm 100:1-2). "For the Lord is good; his mercy is everlasting; and his truth endureth to all generations" (Psalm 100:5). As we try to follow Jesus' teachings, when we stumble along the way, we ask for God's mercy and forgiveness. We all can rejoice in the knowledge that God is merciful. Do you serve the Lord with gladness? What do you need His help with today?

April 13

"For he that will love life, and see good days, let him refrain his tongue from evil, and his lips that they speak no guile: Let him eschew evil, and do good; let him seek peace and ensue it" (1 Peter 3:10-11). Let us be on our guard to speak the truth and not to spread negativity or slander. Let us remember to give compliments when they are appropriate and to support the other people around us. This way lies peace and shows God's love. Who do you know that might need a kind word today? How might you help?

April 14

"Bless the Lord, O my soul: and all that is within me, bless his holy name" (Psalm 103:1). With a glad heart we give thanks to the Lord for each day and for each blessing that we have been given. We give Him the praise and we lean on Him for our strength. What blessings do you have in your life? Give thanks in prayer for each blessing. Thinking of one blessing often reminds us of several more.

April 15

Tax time reminds me of Jesus saying, "Render therefore unto Caesar the things which be Caesar's, and unto God the things which be God's" (Luke 20:25). We give our dues to the government by the law. We give God our all, as everything we are and everything we have is through His blessings and with His help. What talents would you like to develop? How might you use those talents for the Lord? Music? Singing? Reading? Helping others?

April 16

"The Lord is merciful and gracious, slow to anger, and plenteous in mercy" (Psalm 103:8). A prayer: We thank You Lord for Your grace and mercy which are given to us for the asking. Even when we try Your patience, You forgive us when we repent. Help us to stop our sins and to do Thy will. Help us be better servants to Thee. Amen. Can you think of ways to improve your behavior that would be pleasing to the Lord? We are all "works in progress."

April 17

"And the angel answered and said unto the women, Fear not ye: for I know that ye seek Jesus, which was crucified. He is not here: for he is risen, as he said. Come see the place where the Lord lay" (Matthew 28:5-6). This is the good news (or the Gospel) of the

Bible. Jesus died for our sins and rose from the dead to life eternal. We can ask for forgiveness and receive God's grace and mercy. On which ever date Easter is celebrated each year, that good news is true all year long! Hallelujah! Have you said, "Thank You, Jesus" today? Take some time in prayer to show Him a grateful heart.

April 18

Models are usually beautiful or handsome of face and appearance. That type of beauty is superficial (not saying that the person is superficial). Not all of us can hope to be a paid model as a profession – I know I am not in line for that career. Nor do I mind. Beauty that glows from inside, no matter what our superficial look, is the type of beauty which we can all hope for. Knowing God's peace and love makes us all glow with a beauty that is felt and seen and is a strong witness for the Lord. "I will praise thee; for I am fearfully and wonderfully made: marvelous are thy works; and *that* my soul knoweth right well" (Psalm 139:14). Does your love for God show on your face as well as in your actions?

April 19

Having the type of glow mentioned in yesterday's reading comes from our faith in the Lord. Living a life committed to Jesus shows in our actions and makes others say, "I want to be like her!" or "I want what he has!" Through His grace and mercy are we saved, and we come to know His peace and love. Of course, that does not mean that we feel "up" every minute of every day, but even through troubles and problems, we have the Lord by our side. "For with God nothing shall be impossible" (Luke 1:37). Do you have problems at the moment that need prayer? Take time to share them with the Lord.

April 20

"Wherefore take unto you the whole armour of God, that ye may be able to withstand in the evil day, and having done all, to stand" (Ephesians 6:13). When you get up in the mornings and put on clothes, don't forget to also put on the armor of God. Wrap Jesus' love around you just as your very clothes surround you. This way you will be prepared for the day and to meet any challenges that you face. Ask God in prayer to protect you and guide you through your day. Besides yourself, who else would you ask God to protect through this day?

April 21

"And now, little children, abide in him; that, when he shall appear, we may have confidence, and not be ashamed before him at his coming" (1 John 2:28). We need to stay in contact with Jesus through prayer, so that He will know us when He returns. And so that we will be ready for Him whenever or however we meet Him. Do you have a habit of praying each day? Do you say quick prayers during the day whenever you have a need to lean on Jesus' strength? Now is a good time to develop the habit of prayer.

April 22

When the two women came to the place of Jesus' tomb and were told by the angel that He is risen and that they were to go tell the disciples this, the Bible tells us: "And they departed quickly from the sepulcher with fear and great joy; and did run to bring his disciples word" (Matthew 28:8). I can imagine both the fear and great joy that they felt. What awesome news. And what awesome faith the women show. They do not stop to question or argue. They go immediately to do the angels biding. I hope I would do the same. Would you?

April 23

Who is the center of your universe? Some people think it is themselves. God is the creator of the universe and the center of the universe. If we live our lives in this knowledge, we will be more balanced and more in tune with His will for our lives. As we follow His will, we feel more satisfaction and fulfillment in our lives. "O Lord, how manifold are thy works! in wisdom hast thou made them all: the earth is full of thy riches" (Psalm 104:24).

April 24

You are loved. Jesus loves you so much that He died for you. When you know Him, you will love Him back. Let Him into your heart and life. If you do not yet know Him, reading the Bible, especially the New Testament is a good place to start. Prayer, Bible study, church attendance or talking with other Christians are good ways to come to a closer relationship with Him. "Cause me to hear thy lovingkindness in the morning; for in thee do I trust: cause me to know the way wherein I should walk; for I lift up my soul unto thee" (Psalm 143:8). If you do know Him, share His love with those around you. Is there anyone you know that you might want to invite to come to church with you? How else might you share His love?

April 25

"Teach me to do thy will; for thou art my God: thy spirit is good; lead me into the land of uprightness" (Psalm 143:10). A prayer: Jesus we ask You to be near us always and to help us know Your will for our lives. Give us strength to do Your will and forgive us our sins. Help us to follow Your commandment to love one another. We lift our hearts to You and thank You for all You have done for us. Amen. What blessings do you have to be thankful for today? Do you always recognize a blessing at the time it occurs?

April 26

"Surely goodness and mercy shall follow me all the days of my life: and I will dwell in the house of the Lord for ever" (Psalm 23:6). What comfort it is to know that God's mercy is there for us, just for the asking. Ask for mercy and forgiveness through prayer and God grants us His mercy and grace. There is power in prayer. What do you need to pray for today?

April 27

"The Lord is my light and my salvation; whom shall I fear? the Lord is the strength of my life; of whom shall I be afraid?" (Psalm

27:1). A prayer: Lord, we ask your protection for our loved ones throughout this day. Be with us all now and forever, we pray. Help us to be good servants to You. Show us Your will for our lives. Thank You for all the blessings You have given to us. In Jesus' name we pray. Amen. What are some things that you can do to be a good servant to the Lord?

April 28

The Bible tells us that Jesus told His disciples, "I am the way, the truth, and the life: no man cometh unto the Father, but by me" (John 14:6). Nourish (feed) your spiritual life by drawing closer to Jesus. Prayer, Bible study, doing His work by helping others, and quietly listening to Jesus are all ways to come closer to Him. Can you think of some other ways?

April 29

"Praise ye the Lord. Praise the Lord, O my soul" (Psalm 146:1). Praise Him in good times and in bad times. He is Lord of all and can help you through anything. Many times we learn valuable lessons through hardships. That doesn't make it any easier, but be sure not to miss the lesson for dwelling on the problem. How you solve problems and endure hardships builds your character. Build strong character by listening to Jesus and relying on Him. What life lessons have you learned through hardships?

April 30

"Trust in the Lord with all thine heart; and lean not unto thine own understanding. In all thy ways acknowledge him, and he shall direct thy paths" (Proverbs 3:5-6). Lean on Jesus for your daily strength. He knows your needs and what is in your heart. You have only to ask for His help. Look to Jesus to guide, inspire, and protect you. What do you need to ask Jesus for today?

May 1

"But grow in grace, and in the knowledge of our Lord and Savior Jesus Christ. To him be glory both now and forever. Amen" (2 Peter 3:18). Reading the Bible, prayer and church worship services help us gain knowledge of our Lord. Bask in His love, grace and mercy. Witness for the Lord whenever and wherever you can. What might you do to let others know about God's love?

May 2

"I will sing of the mercies of the Lord forever: with my mouth will I make known thy faithfulness to all generations" (Psalm 89:1). Let us be sure that we do sing God's praises and let the generations coming up after us hear the Bible's good news. Children need to learn of Jesus' love and we need to speak up and spread the Word. Is there anyone in your life that needs to hear the Bible's good news? What could you do to help them learn?

May 3

James 1:22 says, in part "Be ye doers of the word, and not hearers only". Some ways to be a doer:
- Help other people.
- Love your neighbor as yourself.
- Follow the 10 commandments.
- Spread the Word and the love of God.

How else might you be a doer of the Word?

May 4

"The Lord is nigh unto them that are of a broken heart; and saveth such as be of a contrite spirit" (Psalm 34:18). Jesus knows when we are sad and wants to draw near to us. It is likely that we will know some sadness at some point in life. Having Jesus' shoulder to cry on is a great help. Pour out your heart to Him in prayer in times of sadness as well as times of joy. Is anything making you sad today? If so, have you shared it in prayer? Remember all of your blessings too. Recounting all of your blessings often does away with sadness.

May 5

"Bless the Lord, O my soul. O Lord my God, thou art very great; thou art clothed with honour and majesty" (Psalm 104:1). God is good. We are so blessed that this is true. Even when we go astray, He welcomes us back when we turn away from sin and are sorry. His grace and mercy have no end. Praise His name! Is there any behavior in your life that you want to change? Ask Jesus for His help with growing in Christian behavior.

May 6

Jesus is our Savior and Redeemer. His love for us is so great that He died to redeem us from our sins. We can show our love for Him by caring for each other. Sometimes caring just means giving a kind word to someone who needs it, or including someone on the sidelines into a group activity. Sharing a smile, saying hello, or noticing when someone is feeling down is also caring for each other. Share the love of Jesus whenever you can. "And we know that all things work together for good to them that love God, to them who are the called according to his purpose" (Romans 8:28). How do you show that you care for others in your daily life?

May 7

Jesus tells us to forgive each other. We are not meant to hold grudges against each other. That kind of mean spirited feeling harms the one who clings to it. Even if what happened was clearly someone's fault, we need to step back and let go of the ill will. You will feel better yourself for not holding on to bad feelings. No, life is not fair, but how you handle the unfairness affects your life. In Luke 6:36-37, Jesus tells us, "Be ye therefore merciful, as your Father also is merciful. Judge not, and ye shall not be judged: condemn not, and ye shall not be condemned: forgive, and ye shall be forgiven." Is there someone that you need to forgive in your heart? Ask Jesus for His help in forgiving them.

May 8

"I wait for the Lord, my soul doeth wait, and in his word do I hope" (Psalm 130:5). The words of the Bible of faith, hope, charity and love surround us with peace. Let us read His Word and be filled with His love. And let us share that peace and love with others. Do your actions show that you have faith in God? How might you show others that you follow Jesus?

May 9

"Watch therefore: for ye know not what hour your Lord doth come" (Matthew 24:42). No one can predict the second coming of Jesus. If we are near to Him already through prayer, and repenting our sins, we are ready regardless of when it might be. Keep your prayer life and spiritual life nurtured always, so that you might welcome Him whenever it will be. What else might you do to strengthen your faith?

May 10

"When thou saidst, Seek ye my face; my heart said unto thee, Thy face, Lord, will I seek" (Psalm 27:8). Seek Him through worship services, song, Bible reading, fellowship with other Christians, prayer, thought, word and deed. What other ways can you think of to seek God? "Blessed are they that keep his testimonies, and that seek him with the whole heart" (Psalm 119:2).

May 11

"Verily I say unto you, Inasmuch as ye have done it unto one of the least of these my brethren, ye have done it unto me" (Matthew 25:40 in part). Our deeds do not go unnoticed by God. The Bible tells us that He considers our acts of kindness to others as acts of kindness to Him. Helping to feed and clothe those without resources, or to visit those who are alone, or to minister to anyone in need, are all deeds done for the Lord. Where can you be of help today?

May 12

"And this commandment have we from him, That he who loveth God love his brother also" (1 John 4:21). This is not always easy to do. When other people are behaving in a manner that we do not like, we need to remember that we still need to love the person even though we do not love their behavior. Showing them this difference can also change the way that person acts toward you. They may be willing to change their behavior if they see that you are objecting to their behavior, not to the person themselves. How might you show someone that you still love them, but you do not love some of their actions? Just telling them is a start. What other ways can you think of?

May 13

"And thou shalt love the Lord thy God with all thine heart, and with all thy soul, and with all thy might" (Deuteronomy 6:5). Every day in every way, we turn to Jesus for advice and for Him to guide us. We can express our love of God through prayer and through our interactions with others. Treating others with love and compassion, in Jesus' name and for His sake, is a way of showing God's love to the world. How do you show in your daily life that you love God?

May 14

"Behold, I stand at the door, and knock: if any man hear my voice, and open the door, I will come in to him, and will sup with him, and he with me" (Revelation 3:20). Jesus tells us that He is near to us and that we have only to open the door to Him. Forgiveness of sins, grace, mercy and undying love are ours for the asking. Awesome! Have you asked Jesus into your life? Ask right now if you haven't yet.

May 15

The word "Pentecost" means 50th in Greek and referred to an annual day set aside for an initial harvest feast. Seven weeks after Jesus arose from the dead, on the day of Pentecost the apostles were filled with the Holy Spirit, as Jesus had told them would happen. Acts 2:1 says, "And when the day of Pentecost was fully come, they were all with one accord in one place." Acts 2:4 says in part, "And they were all filled with the Holy Ghost." There were people from all around present for the feast with many different languages. The apostles spoke to them and each heard the message in their own language. This was described as the apostles speaking in tongues. Thousands of people heard the apostles, became believers and were baptized. Pentecost is celebrated seven weeks after Easter (Easter day + 49 days = 50th day) so falls on a different date each year. God the Father, God the Son and God the Holy Spirit are called the Trinity (the three). What day does Pentecost fall on this year? How might you share God's Word on Pentecost day?

May 16

The Bible tells us that Jesus said, "And he that sent me is with me: the Father hath not left me alone; for I do always those things that please him" (John 8:29). Let us also try to do the things which please God. Also, let us remember that God is always available to us for the asking. Open your heart and let Him in. What are some things that you might do to please God? Think of some things that you already do and some that you may want to do in the future.

May 17

"And Jesus went about all Galilee, teaching in their synagogues, and preaching the gospel of the kingdom, and healing all manner of disease among the people" (Matthew 4:23). The New Testament is full of examples of Jesus healing the lame, the blind, the sick and even raising the dead (Lazarus raised from the dead – see John 11:43-44). He has compassion for us. Talk to Him in prayer to ease illness, whether it be physical or emotional, He is there for you. What healing do you need in your life?

May 18

"And I say unto you, Ask, and it shall be given you; seek, and ye shall find; knock, and it shall be opened unto you" (Luke 11:9). Seek God's forgiveness, grace and mercy and you will find it. Seek the love of God and His peace and you will find it. This doesn't necessarily mean life will be easy, but it does mean you will have help to get through it. What help do you need today? Ask for God's help in prayer.

May 19

I have heard people say that no one knows exactly how someone else feels. If you know the person, you may sometimes have a good idea. However, Jesus always knows exactly how we feel. Who better to turn to and share your sorrow, grief, joy or even anger. He knows and can comfort you. Be not afraid to share your feelings through prayer and receive His help with dealing with those feelings. "I sought the Lord, and he heard me, and delivered me from all my fears" (Psalm 34:4). What feelings or fears do you have that you need help with? Have you talked them over with the Lord in prayer?

May 20

"...but God is faithful, who will not suffer you to be tempted above that ye are able; but will with the temptation also make a way to escape, that ye may be able to bear it" (1 Corinthians 10:13 in part). We face many temptations in this life, but God is there with us. Cling to Him, ask for His help and strength to get you through. He is able to deliver us from evil. Celebrate your victories in praise and worship of Him. What are some temptations that you have resisted? What other temptations do you face? Have you asked God for strength to resist them?

May 21

"Whosoever shall receive this child in my name receiveth me: and whosoever shall receive me receiveth him that sent me…" (Luke 9:48 in part). Jesus wants us to help each other in this world. And there are many different ways to do so. Your time, talents, skills or ideas can all be used for those in need, or those younger than you who just need to learn and grow. Helping children grow in spirit and knowledge of Jesus is a priceless gift. Who in your life might need your help? What ways can you think of to help them?

May 22

"Beloved, follow not that which is evil, but that which is good. He that doeth good is of God: but he that doeth evil hath not seen God" (3 John 1:11). When we look up to people that we admire, we need to be sure not to accept everything they do as correct just because we like them. People are human and none of us are perfect. Choose your role models wisely and do not blanketly approve everything they may do or say. Our greatest, strongest, perfect role model is Jesus. Do you have other role models in addition to Jesus? How do their actions compare with Jesus' teachings?

May 23

"Know ye that the Lord he is God: it is he that hath made us, and not we ourselves; we are his people, and the sheep of his pasture" (Psalm 100:3). We often need to be reminded not to rely only on our own thoughts, but to ask for God's help. Do you ask Him in prayer to lead you in His path? A prayer: Lord we give thanks that You are our shepherd. Lead us in the path of righteousness. Help us to know Your will and to do Your will. Give us strength to follow You. In Jesus' name and for His sake we pray. Amen.

May 24

"Behold, God is my salvation; I will trust, and not be afraid: for the Lord JEHOVAH is my strength and my song; he also is become my salvation" (Isaiah 12:2). How do you show that you trust in the Lord? Thought? Word? Actions? All are good ways. A prayer: We praise You, Lord, for all the blessings You have provided for us. We trust in You to lead us today and every day in the path You have chosen for us. Our hearts are full of songs of praise to You. Forgive us our sins. Thank You for Your grace and mercy. In Jesus' name. Amen.

May 25

"The Lord is righteous in all his ways, and holy in all his works (Psalm 145:17). Even when we do not understand what is happening, we can know that God does. Lean on His strength and pray for His support through hard times. Life sometimes does not make sense to us, but God will get us through it if we ask for His help. What do you need help with today? Ask for God's will to be done.

May 26

"Then Jesus said, Father, forgive them; for they know not what they do" (Luke 23:34 in part). Jesus loved us so much that He could forgive us, even from the very cross. The magnitude of this goodness, this depth of feeling, this love, this miracle is beyond my understanding. I am humbled, grateful, certainly undeserving, and very thankful for Jesus' sacrifice. I will try to be a good servant with His help. Have you said, "Thank You, Lord" for this miracle of His love? In what ways do you try to be a good servant to the Lord?

May 27

"I will praise thee, O Lord my God, with all my heart: and I will glorify thy name for evermore" (Psalm 86:12). Do you praise God when you receive His blessings? Do you let Him know when you feel thankful for something? A prayer: We thank You, Lord, for the blessings we receive. We thank You for the opportunities we are given. Help us walk in the path that You have set for us. Give us the strength to do Your will. Thine be the glory. Amen.

May 28

"Blessed are they which do hunger and thirst after righteousness: for they shall be filled" (Matthew 5:6). Seek for God to guide you and for Him to inspire you in all that you do. We want to do the right thing in our daily lives. If we know the Bible, we stand a better chance of knowing what the right thing is. At times when it isn't that clear, take it to the Lord in prayer. What questions do you have in your life today?

May 29

"Come unto me, all ye that labour and are heavy laden, and I will give you rest" (Matthew 11:28). Life gets us down sometimes. We may not feel that we understand what is going on, or why. It is important to know that God is in control and we will not necessarily understand. But we need to have faith and continue doing our best while asking for the Lord's help. Keep your faith strong. Bolster your prayer life and look for the life lessons. What is God teaching you right now?

May 30

"Thy word have I hid in mine heart, that I might not sin against thee" (Psalm 119:11). Be always aware of your actions in light of God's Word. Are you following His commandments? When you have choices to make, be sure you consider what God wants you to do. Pray for Him to guide you and for His strength. What choices are you facing right now? How will your choices fit into God's commandments?

May 31

"Greater love hath no man than this, that a man lay down his life for his friends" (John 15:13). On Memorial Day we remember those in the military who died serving our country, protecting and defending our freedom. We ask God to bless our troops, and protect them. We pray for God to guide our leaders, that they may follow God's will and take us in the direction that He would have us go. We thank God that Jesus died for all of us and was raised to live again. What else are you thankful for on this day?

June 1

The Bible tells us that Jesus said, "These things I have spoken unto you, that in me ye might have peace. In the world ye shall have tribulation: but be of good cheer; I have overcome the world" (John 16:33). Because we know Jesus, does not mean that we will not have any troubles, but it does mean that He will help us through. Lift your troubles to Him in prayer. Take comfort in the fact that He knows our problems and will help us. What problems do you have today? Take them to the Lord.

June 2

"Seek the Lord, and his strength: seek his face evermore" (Psalm 105:4). If you are seeking to know Jesus, then you are on the right path. Seek for Him to guide you in living your life. Seek His mercy and forgiveness of your sins. Seek His protection as you go through your day. And seek to share your faith with others. How might you share Jesus' love with others?

June 3

Jesus gives us the Lord's Prayer: "After this manner therefore pray ye: Our Father which art in heaven, Hallowed be thy name" (Matthew 6:9). Jesus is teaching us how to pray. God is our Father and is to be deeply respected. He is holy, sacred and we are His children. How wonderful for us that God loves us. We are blessed beyond belief. Did you know that when we say the Lord's Prayer, we are using words that Jesus Himself gave us all those years ago? It is awesome to think how many people have repeated Jesus' direct words. How do your actions show reverence to the Lord?

June 4

The Lord's Prayer continued. "Thy kingdom come. Thy will be done in earth, as it is in heaven" (Matthew 6:10). What a wonderful place heaven must be. If we would all follow God's will we would see a bit of heaven here on earth. Our sinful condition keeps us from measuring up, but we can try to do our best. How might you behave in a way that lets people know that you are a child of God?

June 5

The Lord's Prayer continued. "Give us this day our daily bread" (Matthew 6:11). We are being told to look to God each day for our support and nourishment, day by day. Take one day at a time. Just as we need food to nourish our body we also need prayer to nourish our soul. Do you have a certain time of the day to say your daily prayers? If not, chose a time and begin to develop the habit. Nourish your daily prayer life. Feed your faith.

June 6

The Lord's Prayer continued. "And forgive us our debts, as we forgive our debtors" (Matthew 6:12). As God forgives us, we are to also forgive other people. God forgives us even though we don't deserve it. We need to remember that and forgive each other too, deserving or not. This may be hard to do. Pray for the strength to forgive if you are having trouble letting go of something. Is there anyone in your life that you need to forgive? If so, pray for the strength to do so.

June 7

The Lord's Prayer continued. "And lead us not into temptation, but deliver us from evil: For thine is the kingdom, and the power, and the glory, forever. Amen" (Matthew 6:13). There are many temptations along the path of our lives. We need God's help to resist temptation and to stay away from evil. Our hope is to one day come into His kingdom, through His grace and mercy. What a glorious day that will be! What temptations are you facing today? Have you developed the habit of asking Jesus to help you through your challenges?

June 8

"Fear thou not; for I am with thee: be not dismayed; for I am thy God: I will strengthen thee; yea, I will help thee; yea, I will uphold thee with the right hand of my righteousness" (Isaiah 41:10). What a comfort it is to know that God cares for us. We have His strength to lean on to carry us through. We don't have to go it alone, God is with us. Hallelujah! What things do you need His help with this day?

June 9

"And whosoever will be chief among you, let him be your servant: Even as the Son of man came not to be ministered unto, but to minister, and to give his life a ransom for many" (Matthew 20:27-28). Jesus spent His life in service of others, healing, teaching and showing us by example just how He wanted us to treat each other. We can follow that example by helping wherever we see a need and by praying for each other. Where do you see chances to help other people in your life?

June 10

Sometimes we wonder just how we will ever get through the hardship or trials that we are facing. God knows our troubles though, and will help us through. Pray for Him to guide you and for His strength. Take each day step by step and lean on His power. Look to Him for the right path through your challenges. "And he said unto me, My grace is sufficient for thee: for my strength is made perfect in weakness" (2 Corinthians 12:9 in part). What troubles do you need His help with today?

June 11

"But seek ye first the kingdom of God, and his righteousness; and all these things shall be added unto you" (Matthew 6:33). Jesus tells us in His sermon on the mount that God knows that we need to be clothed and fed. But the important thing is to seek His kingdom and not to become bogged down in the less important things in life. Look at your priorities and be sure you are putting Jesus first. Where in your life might you need to make some changes to put Jesus first?

June 12

"Jesus Christ the same yesterday, and to day, and for ever" (Hebrews 13:8). Jesus does not change. We do not need to worry that He will feel differently about us from day to day. He loves us and wants us to walk with Him all the days of our lives. His rules/commandments do not change from one day to another. We have consistent boundaries and consistent love. This is reason to rejoice! Do your interactions with other people follow Jesus' commandments to love one another? What are some examples of that?

June 13

"O God, thou knowest my foolishness; and my sins are not hid from thee" (Psalm 69:5). God knows us inside and out, and loves us anyway! Hallelujah for His amazing grace! That is our comfort and our joy. We can count on Him to accept our repentance of our sins and forgive us. To repent of something means to be sorry that you did that something. It also means that you wish you had not done it and that you will not do it again. It does not mean that you are just sorry you got caught – it means you are truly sorry you did it to begin with. When you ask forgiveness, be sure you mean it. Do you have anything on your mind that you need to take to the Lord in prayer?

June 14

"Let all those that seek thee rejoice and be glad in thee: and let such as love thy salvation say continually, Let God be magnified" (Psalm 70:4). We continually rejoice that God is merciful to us. We praise His name for the many blessings He gives to us. Praise the Lord with a glad and grateful heart! What things are you thankful for today? Let the Lord know, in prayer.

June 15

"Let the heavens be glad, and let the earth rejoice: and let men say among the nations, The Lord reigneth" (1 Chronicles 16:31).
Thank You for this beautiful earth
Help us, Lord, to realize the worth
Of each day that You give us
And each chance to be of service.
Through these long summer days
Let us rejoice always
As we bask in the sun
And enjoy our summer fun.
Smell the beautiful flowers,
Sing Your praises for hours.
You bless us with mercy and grace
We thank You for our earthly place. Amen.

What do you like best about God's glorious summer creations?

June 16

Once in a while it is good to take stock of your life. What are the good things/people/situations in your life? Nurture and nourish that which is good and thank God for each blessing. Be sure you take time to let those people know that you appreciate them. Give time to those situations that need bolstering. What are the bad or unhealthy things or issues/situations in your life? Ask God how to deal with those and how He would have you resolve those issues. Staying God-centered helps you stay on track. "And we know that all things work together for good to them that love God, to them who are the called according to His purpose" (Romans 8:28).

June 17

"I will say of the Lord, He is my refuge and my fortress: my God; in him will I trust" (Psalm 91:2). A prayer: We thank You, Lord, for the many blessings which You have supplied for us. Help us share our blessings with others and help us to share Your Word. We trust You to guide us and pray You will make known Your will in our lives. Forgive us our sins and help us be better servants for You. In Jesus' name. Amen. What blessings has God given to you? Have you recognized them and said, "Thank You" in prayer?

June 18

I have had jobs that I loved and jobs that I did not love. I always thanked the Lord for whatever job I had at the moment, though, because I knew that not everyone was fortunate enough to have a job at all. Even if your circumstances need improvement, you can thank the Lord for what you do have and ask that He help you make those improvements, if it is within His will for your life. And ask for strength to deal with the circumstances day by day. His strength will carry you through. "He giveth power to the faint; and to them that have no might he increaseth strength" (Isaiah 40:29). What are you thankful for today? What do you need God's strength to help you deal with?

June 19

"Praise ye the Lord. Praise, O ye servants of the Lord, praise the name of the Lord. Blessed be the name of the Lord from this time forth and for evermore" (Psalm 113:1-2). The wondrous works of the Lord are all around us every day. Sometimes we forget to notice things like sunshine, flowers, beautiful rainbows, or birds singing in the trees. Children laughing and playing, older people sitting in the park in the sunshine, people going about their daily business. All beautiful in their own way, and all God's handiwork. What joys do you see around about you today?

June 20

"Then I called upon the name of the Lord; O Lord, I beseech thee, deliver my soul. Gracious is the Lord, and righteous; yea, our God is merciful" (Psalm 116:4-5). Such an honor to be able to call upon the Lord. We are truly blessed. Let us remember to call on the Lord through our prayers both in times of need and in times of joy. Let us remember to say, "Thank You" as often as we say, "Help me." God is good! What are you thankful for today?

June 21

"Thy word is a lamp unto my feet, and a light unto my path" (Psalm 119:105). Our roadmap through life is the Bible. The commandments are our user's manual. Look to "The Good Book" when you have questions. And contact technical support through "knee mail" (prayer). Let your thoughts, words and deeds show that you live for the Lord. How do your actions show in your life that you follow Jesus?

June 22

"Depart from me, ye evildoers: for I will keep the commandments of my God" (Psalm 119:115). If you become tempted to behave in a way that you do not feel is correct – recite this verse to yourself to draw the strength to resist temptation. There are many temptations in this world and we need God's strength to help us remain true to His commandments. God is with you. What temptations do you face today? Ask God to help you through the day.

June 23

"And the prayer of faith shall save the sick, and the Lord shall raise him up; and if he have committed sins, they shall be forgiven him" (James 5:15). In times of illness, turn to Jesus for help with healing. He is certainly able to support you through whatever you have to deal with. Always ending with, "Thy will be done, not mine" as Jesus knows what is best for your life. Whether He heals you from illness or supports you through it, He will be by your side. Never underestimate the power of prayer. What do you need to pray for today?

June 24

"I will extol thee, my God, O King; and I will bless thy name for ever and ever. Every day will I bless thee; and I will praise thy name for ever and ever" (Psalm 145:1-2). Let us show through our thoughts, words and actions that we praise Jesus' name. Let us pass along the peace of Christ to other people at every opportunity. Let us give thanks in prayer every day. How do you show to the world that you love the Lord?

June 25

"Draw nigh to God, and he will draw nigh to you. Cleanse your hands, ye sinners; and purify your hearts, ye double minded" (James 4:8). Ways to draw near to God: Prayer, praise, singing, worshiping together with others, quiet reflection alone, listening to gospel music, reading the Bible, helping one another, being there for someone who needs you. What other ways do you think of to draw near to God?

June 26

"Humble yourselves in the sight of the Lord, and he shall lift you up" (James 4:10). Being humble in prayer helps us to admit that we need help. Being humble in public helps us to relate to others in a way that encourages them to open up to us. Being humble helps us avoid sinful pride. Are there areas of your life where you might need to be more humble? How might you show humbleness?

June 27

"Then spake Jesus again unto them, saying, I am the light of the world: he that followeth me shall not walk in darkness, but shall have the light of life" (John 8:12). Did you ever notice that when you keep Jesus at your side during your walk through life that you feel more confident and content? Darkness and unsure feelings can creep in when we forget to keep Jesus near through our day. Pray without ceasing!

June 28

In the Bible, Jesus tells us, "…lo, I am with you alway, even unto the end of the world" (Matthew 28:20 in part). We can share our joys and our sorrows by means of prayer, and always know that the love and comfort of Jesus is with us. Pouring out our feelings, our fears, our joys and delights through prayer helps us to stay close to Jesus. Yes, He already knows what is going on in your life. Putting it into your own words and sharing the joy increases that joy. Asking for help with a problem brings the problem into focus. When you ask for help remember to listen for the answer. Do you share your day with Jesus in prayer?

June 29

"With my whole heart have I sought thee: O let me not wander from thy commandments" (Psalm 119:10). Do you remember to match your actions to Jesus' commandments? A prayer: Lord, we seek to do Your will. We want to obey Your commandments. Help us to walk with You every day. Lead us in the path You would have us follow. Use our talents in Your service. In Jesus' name. Amen.

June 30

"I will praise the Lord according to his righteousness: and will sing praise to the name of the Lord most high" (Psalm 7:17). Praise the Lord for all the blessings He has given you. Let Him know through prayer that you are thankful for His help and presence in your life. Thinking about our blessings and giving thanks makes us even more aware of all that God has done for us. What has God done for you? What can you do for God?

July 1

"And he said unto them, Go ye into all the world, and preach the gospel to every creature" (Mark 16:15). Are you able to witness for the Lord in your everyday life? You don't have to be in church at the moment to be a witness for Jesus. If you see a friend having problems, you might remind them that Jesus is as near as a prayer. Or inviting someone to attend church with you, is being a witness for God. There are many simple, small things you could do that might just turn out to be something big for others around you. Think of some things you might do in your daily life to witness for the Lord. Let your light so shine!

July 2

"Let the people praise thee, O God; let all the people praise Thee. O let nations be glad and sing for joy: for thou shalt judge the people righteously, and govern the nations upon the earth" (Psalm 67:3-4 in part). As we pray, let us include our government leaders and our country, as well as all countries on the earth. Pray that our leaders seek God's advice and follow His will. Do you know who your congressmen or congresswomen and representatives are? Have you ever written to them to express your opinion about an issue? We can encourage them to seek God's will and ask for Him to guide their decisions.

July 3

"O praise the Lord, all ye nations: praise him all ye people. For his merciful kindness is great toward us: and the truth of the Lord endureth for ever. Praise ye the Lord" (Psalm 117:1-2). As a nation we need to protect our religious freedom to worship God without fear. We need to make our voices heard to our leaders in support of our individual freedoms and not let the voices of a few people outweigh the majority. God stands with us when we stand up for Him. What are some freedoms that we take for granted that some other countries do not have?

July 4

"Blessed is the nation whose God is the Lord" (Psalm 33:12 in part).
Lord keep our country strong, we pray
Help us through each night and day.
Help us always turn to You
Keep us ever strong and true.
Teach us how to love each other
To treat each person as our brother.
Teach us to be helpful and giving
As Jesus taught us through His living. Amen.

In what ways do you show that you follow Jesus' teachings?

July 5

"Blessed is the man that endureth temptation: for when he is tried, he shall receive the crown of life, which the Lord hath promised to those that love him" (James 1:12). Stay strong in your faith and resist temptations. Ask God for His help and His strength. Recognizing when you need help and asking for help are very important factors in resisting temptations. What temptations do you face? And how do you handle those situations?

July 6

"For thou art my hope, O Lord God: thou art my trust from my youth" (Psalm 71:5). We can trust in the Lord to help us with our problems. Things become more manageable when we share them with God and put our trust in Him to guide us. Seek His will for your life. What problems do you need to talk over with the Lord?

July 7

"Beloved, let us love one another: for love is of God; and every one that loveth is born of God, and knoweth God" (1 John 4:7). Do you show love in your daily interactions with other people? Respect and support for each other goes a long way to bringing people together in peace. A simple smile or a helping hand can be that first step to showing God's love to others. What other ways do you think of to share God's love with others?

July 8

"Go ye therefore, and teach all nations, baptizing them in the name of the Father, and of the Son, and of the Holy Ghost" (Matthew 28:19). Jesus instructed His disciples to spread the gospel to all nations. We can also do our small part by sharing the gospel within our own community. Who do you know that needs to hear the gospel? How might you participate in an outreach program? Simply inviting someone to a church service is a start.

July 9

The Bible tells us that Jesus said, "For whosoever shall do the will of God, the same is my brother, and my sister and mother" (Mark 3:35). We are all God's children. Differences in our looks do not matter. It is what is in our hearts and our actions, as we do the will of God, that brings us together. Can people see in your actions that you are a child of God? What else might you do to show that you follow Jesus?

July 10

"For what shall it profit a man, if he shall gain the whole world, and lose his own soul?" (Mark 8:36). Think of this verse when you have decisions to make and you are unsure of what to do. It is especially hard when the choices are not clearly right and wrong. Pray for understanding of God's will for your life and for Him to guide your decisions. What decisions do you face today? Have you prayed for God's help?

July 11

The Bible tells us that Jesus said, "Whosoever shall receive one of such children in my name, receiveth me: and whosoever shall receive me, receiveth not me, but him that sent me" (Mark 9:37).

Whenever you do a good deed to anyone, you are doing a good deed for Jesus. He tells us to help those in need, in His name. Having compassion on us, He also wants us to have compassion for each other. You can make a difference in someone's life with your outreach and compassion. Have you shown compassion to others in your life? Is there anyone you know who needs your compassion right now?

July 12

"Behold, how good and how pleasant it is for brethren to dwell together in unity!" (Psalm 133:1). Getting along well with others can be difficult at times. Especially when there are sharp differences of opinion and when people behave in ways of which we do not approve. Talking over the situation calmly and rationally is preferable to getting angry and not listening to another's point of view. Pray for strength to be able to resolve your conflicts peaceably. What conflicts do you have in your life at present?

July 13

"But Noah found grace in the eyes of the Lord" (Genesis 6:8). This simple sentence is so profound. God was so disappointed with us that He was about to give up on us. But Noah found grace in the eyes of the Lord. Noah must have felt surrounded by wickedness, yet he persevered in his beliefs. Noah listened to God and built the ark even when there was no sign yet of the floods to come. We must also continue to serve God even if we feel alone in doing so. Spread His Word at every opportunity and remember that Jesus is always with you. You never know who may be watching you and being lead to the Lord through you. Will you be as trusting as Noah if God leads you to do something?

July 14

"And as ye would that men should do to you, do ye also to them likewise" (Luke 6:31). Often called the Golden Rule, this is how Jesus tells us to interact with one another. It is fairly easy to see when someone else is not following this rule. Do you see any instances in your own life where you have not followed this rule? That is often much harder to see. What might you have done differently to follow the Golden Rule?

July 15

"And whatsoever ye do in word or deed, do all in the name of the Lord Jesus, giving thanks to God and the Father by him" (Colossians 3:17). Our accomplishments come to us through hard work and through developing the talents God gave us. Remember to give Him the praise. What talents do you use for the Lord? What other talents would you like to develop?

July 16

"Continue in prayer, and watch in the same with thanksgiving" (Colossians 4:2). Prayer and thanksgiving go hand in hand. Our prayers concerning sorrow, joy, pain, healing, relationships, fears, illness, comfort, or anything else can also contain thankfulness for our blessings. In the midst of sorrow, our blessings still exist. Acknowledging your blessings may help you through your sorrows. What blessings do you give thanks for this day?

July 17

Through our church groups and worship services, we bolster and support other people. It is important to be able to share our concerns as well as joys. Through the church we can share with fellow members as well as organize to help others outside of our specific congregation. Who would you share this blessing with: "Grace be with you, mercy, and peace, from God the Father, and from the Lord Jesus Christ, the Son of the Father, in truth and love" (2 John 1:3). What joys and concerns do you have right now?

July 18

"And thou shalt do that which is right and good in the sight of the Lord: that it may be well with thee" (Deuteronomy 6:18 in part). If you are contemplating which course of action is best, be sure to ask what the Lord wants of you. Pray for Him to guide you and seek to do that which is right. Often this takes many prayers, as the right thing to do may not be immediately clear. Keep lifting your situation up to the Lord. Once you know what is good in His sight, you have your answer. What do you need help with today?

July 19

"Thou shalt love the Lord thy God with all thy heart, and with all thy soul, and with all thy strength, and with all thy mind; and thy neighbor as thyself" (Luke 10:27 in part). Who is my neighbor? In the parable of the good Samaritan (see Luke 10:30-37), Jesus shows us that we are all neighbors. Even the people you do not know. The Samaritan saw a man in need and he stopped to help even though he did not know the man. Jesus tells us to "Go, and do thou likewise" (Luke 10:37 in part). We need to remember that not knowing someone does not mean that we can't help. Do you have a neighbor in need? What might you do to help?

July 20

"Thou shalt not avenge, nor bear any grudge against the children of thy people, but thou shalt love thy neighbor as thyself: I am the Lord. Ye shall keep my statutes" (Leviticus 19:18-19 in part). Sometimes helping or loving your neighbor may simply involve showing respect to them. Even if we do not see eye to eye on all things, we can still deal with each other in a respectful manner. Creating win-win situations, rather than striving for "I win – you lose" is a good way to show respect and support for others. And others may be lead to Jesus through seeing your actions. Do you show respect for people around you, even when you do not agree with them? How might you show respect even when you disagree?

July 21

"Many, O Lord my God, are thy wonderful works which thou hast done" (Psalm 40:5 in part). All of the beauty in nature speaks to the glory of God. His creations are magnificent. Humbly we realize that we are His creations too and are awesomely made. We tend to take ourselves for granted most of the time. God has given us the capacity to love. He has given each of us different talents. How we develop and use those talents is our gift back to God. What talents or interests would you like to develop?

July 22

"I delight to do thy will, O my God: yea, thy law is within my heart" (Psalm 40:8). We desire to do good. Sometimes we go astray. The more we know about God's Word and the closer we live to Him, the less our chances of going astray. When we study the Bible, and keep His commandments close to our hearts, we keep ourselves in tune with God's will. Do you keep Him close to your heart? How might you show Him that you do?

July 23

"Great is the Lord, and greatly to be praised" (Psalm 48:1 in part). I have shared worship services with a few people in a small church and also with many people in large congregations. Both ways can be very moving. The intimacy of the small gathering swells my heart with God's love. A large crowd singing in joyous unison carries me away and uplifts my very soul. Prayer and praise alone in a quiet spot is also very healing. God is good and greatly to be praised in whatever environment we happen to be in. What is your favorite way to worship God?

July 24

"Create in me a clean heart, O God; and renew a right spirit within me" (Psalm 51:10). What ways do you serve the Lord? A prayer: Lord, help us to be better servants to You. Help us to do that which is pleasing in your sight. We pray for Your guidance and direction as we go through this day. We pray for your protection for ourselves and for our loved ones. Thank You for all You have done for us. In Jesus' name we pray. Amen.

July 25

"Be merciful unto me, O God, be merciful unto me: for my soul trusteth in thee" (Psalm 57:1 in part). We are blessed to be able to call upon the Lord, repent of our sins, and receive His mercy and grace. Jesus died in order for us all to have this greatest gift. The wonder of that love draws us to love Him in return. He is worthy of our trust and love. Have you said a prayer of thankfulness today?

July 26

"I will praise thee, O Lord, among the people: I will sing unto thee among the nations. For thy mercy is great unto the heavens, and thy truth unto the clouds" (Psalm 57:9-10). Praise the Lord for all the blessings He has given to us. Praise God for answered prayer, for the love of family and friends, and for God's love in our lives. What do you praise Him for on this day?

July 27

"Hear my cry, O God; attend to my prayer. From the end of the earth will I cry unto thee, when my heart is overwhelmed: lead me to the rock that is higher than I" (Psalm 61:1-2). When you feel overwhelmed, turn to Jesus in prayer. There is much in this world to deal with and most of us do feel overwhelmed at one time or another. Step by step, with Jesus' help, we can get through anything. What seems overwhelming to you right now?

July 28

"In God is my salvation and my glory: the rock of my strength, and my refuge, is in God. Trust in him at all times; ye people, pour out your heart before him" (Psalm 62:7-8 in part). We are blessed to have the Lord's strength to call upon. We need never be alone, as He is always near. May He comfort and keep you, now and always. What do you need God's strength to help you with today?

July 29

Perspective is key to managing disappointments. The old adage about, "I was sorry I had no shoes, then I met a man who had no feet" shows the importance of perspective. Concentrating on what we do have instead of what we do not have keeps us more balanced. Even when Job was being tested he said, "...the Lord gave, and the Lord hath taken away; blessed be the name of the Lord. In all this Job sinned not, nor charged God foolishly" (Job 1:21-22 in part). In times of troubles we can cling to our relationship with God and trust in Him to see us through. What do you need to gain some perspective with today?

July 30

"Whosoever therefore shall be ashamed of me and of my words...of him also shall the Son of man be ashamed, when he cometh in the glory of his Father with the holy angels" (Mark 8:38 in part). We should never be embarrassed or ashamed to speak up for Jesus. It may be easy in the presence of other known Christians. It may be more difficult when we do not know the people around us. Take a breath and ask Jesus for strength, then speak up in His name. What situations do you need Jesus' help with?

July 31

"And let the peace of God rule in your hearts" (Colossians 3:15 in part). Peace is often elusive in this busy and hectic world. Take time to quiet yourself and communicate with God in prayer. His peace is given to us for the asking. Not that our troubles disappear, but that we become more able to address them with His help and through His strength. What areas of life do you need peace with today?

August 1

"The glory of the Lord shall endure forever: the Lord shall rejoice in his works." "My meditation of him will be sweet: I will be glad in the Lord" (Psalm 104:31 and 34). It is a comforting feeling to be able to talk things over with Jesus in prayer. Always know that you are not alone, and you have the love of Jesus to sustain you. Whatever our problems, He has the answers. He *is* the answer. What problems do you need to take to Him today?

August 2

God answers prayer. Sometimes it does not happen as quickly as we would like. And sometimes it seems to us that our prayers are going unanswered. At those times it is possible the answer was "No" or "Not yet." But if we haven't gotten what we want, it appears that there was no answer. If what we are praying for does not work with God's plan for our lives, the answer might just be "No." We need to keep praying but always end with, "Thy will be done, not mine" and mean it. Pray for the strength to deal with whatever God has in store for your life. "Many are the afflictions of the righteous: but the Lord delivereth him out of them all" (Psalm 34:19). When you pray for help do you listen for God's answers?

August 3

"And blessed be his glorious name for ever: and let the whole earth be filled with his glory; Amen, and Amen" (Psalm 72:19). Whether it be a glorious sunshiny day or a crisp autumn afternoon, the earth declares the glory of the Lord. On those beautiful days where each breath you take has you thankful for just being alive – give thanks to God for His awesome bounty. Hallelujah! Where do you see the beauty of the Lord around you?

August 4

"Trust in him at all times; ye people, pour out your heart before him: God is a refuge for us" (Psalm 62:8 in part). When you don't know where to turn, here is your answer. God is our refuge. We can pour out our hearts and pray for help and understanding. Put your trust in the Lord and lift up your problems to Him. Place yourself in His capable hands. What help do you need today? Pray for the Lord to lead you.

August 5

"Because thy lovingkindness is better than life, my lips shall praise thee" (Psalm 63:3). God's love is available to us anytime and anywhere. His love is never ending and is far more than enough to meet our needs. Walk in faith with Him and you will not walk alone. This gospel truth fills us with hope and makes us want to share the good news with others. How can you share God's love today?

August 6

"God be merciful unto us, and bless us; and cause his face to shine upon us; Se-lah. That thy way may be known upon earth, thy saving health among all nations" (Psalm 67:1-2). Go through this day with a smile in your heart and on your face. The important thing is that God is with you. Everything else can be dealt with, with His help. Call upon the Lord to carry you through, day by day. What problems do you need God's help with today?

August 7

"The Lord is good to all: and his tender mercies are over all his works. All thy works shall praise thee, O Lord; and thy saints shall bless thee" (Psalm 145:9-10). Let our hearts and tongues be filled with praise for the Lord. God is good, God is able, God is near. Share His Word, share His praise, share your day with Him. Who would you like to share God's love with today? How might you do that?

August 8

"Charity suffereth long, and is kind; charity envieth not; charity vaunteth not itself, is not puffed up" (1 Corinthians 13:4). Charity and humility make a great combination. Giving to others from a kind heart with the motive of seeing others meet their needs is a pure motive. Giving to others in order to be seen in a good light yourself is an impure motive. Being human, our instincts often lead us to want praise for what we do. But we need to be sure we are doing good for the sake of others and in Jesus' name, and giving the praise to Him. You can still feel good about it, just not to the extreme of sinful pride. Give the praise to the Lord and store up your own treasures in Heaven. What good deeds would you like to do today?

August 9

"But let the righteous be glad; let them rejoice before God: yea, let them exceedingly rejoice" (Psalm 68:3). If you are a parent, think about how good it makes you feel when your children give you a compliment. Or children, do you notice your parent's broad smiles when you say something good about them? Try giving each family member a compliment today. Imagine how God, our Father, feels when we worship and rejoice in Him. Let us sing His praises all the day long!

August 10

"Hear me, O Lord; for thy lovingkindness is good: turn unto me according to the multitude of thy tender mercies" (Psalm 69:16). God hears our prayers, whether spoken or unspoken. He knows what is in our hearts before we speak. Yet, we still need to pray so that we can commune with God of our own free will. It also helps us to put into our own words what is going on in our lives. Although, at times we are too overwhelmed to be able to put feelings into words. At those times we can just say so, and lift the situation up to the Lord. Ask for His help to cope with overwhelming circumstances. What would you pray for today?

August 11

"Let my mouth be filled with thy praise and with thy honour all the day" (Psalm 71:8). There are many opportunities during the day to praise the Lord. When someone asks how you are, instead of just, "Very well" you might say "Very well, thank the Lord.' Just a small way of keeping God near and letting others know that you do. Take the small opportunities and larger ones will come naturally too. How else might you bring the Lord into your day?

August 12

"But it is good for me to draw near to God: I have put my trust in the Lord God, that I may declare all thy works" (Psalm 73:28). Being Christian is a choice you make. Choose to do it right and to the fullest. Draw near to God in every aspect of your life. Trust in Him and share His Word. Praise the Lord! Do you share God's love with others wherever you can? How might you do so more often?

August 13

"Bow down thine ear, O Lord, hear me: for I am poor and needy" (Psalm 86:1). No matter what material possessions we have, we are all poor and needy before the Lord. When we admit this, and come to Him humbly, we can communicate freely. Rely on God's strength, seek His love, compassion, and His amazing grace. What needs do you have to pray for today? Humbly lift them to the Lord.

August 14

"Be merciful unto me, O Lord: for I cry unto thee daily. Rejoice the soul of thy servant: for unto thee, O Lord, do I lift up my soul" (Psalm 86:3-4). We can rejoice that God gives us His grace and mercy when we have faith in Jesus and ask for forgiveness for our sins. When we walk on life's journey hand in hand with Jesus, we have comfort in His strength. Whatever problems we meet, He will see us through. What problems do you need His help with today?

August 15

"For thou art great, and doest wondrous things: thou art God alone. Teach me thy way, O Lord; I will walk in thy truth: unite my heart to fear thy name" (Psalm 86:10-11). Seek to know God's will for your life. Walk the path He desires for you and keep Him near you. Seek His peace that passes understanding. Have you asked Jesus' help with your life path?

August 16

"The Lord reigneth; let the earth rejoice; let the multitude of isles be glad thereof" (Psalm 97:1). Let us remember that the entire world belongs to God. It is not up to us to judge others, but we have been charged with spreading the Gospel. There are many different ways to worship God but there are also false prophets. So, we need to have a strong knowledge of the Bible in order not to be lead astray, and in order to share His Word correctly. Pray for wisdom and understanding. Who would you like to share God's Word with today?

August 17

"Rejoice in the Lord, ye righteous; and give thanks at the remembrance of his holiness" (Psalm 97:12). Holy is the Lord, and wholeheartedly do we praise His name. With a thankful heart we recognize all the blessings we have received. Humbly we also recognize that we could do more to spread God's Word and share His love. What could you do to share His love with those around you?

August 18

"Great is our Lord, and of great power: his understanding is infinite" (Psalm 147 verse 5). When we don't understand, we can rely on God because He always does. Lean on Him and trust that He will help you. Lift your troubles or sorrows to Him. Lift your joys and thankfulness also. Great is our Lord and greatly to be praised! What troubles would you lift to the Lord in prayer?

August 19

"As ye have therefore received Christ Jesus the Lord, so walk ye in him: rooted and built up in him, and stablished in the faith, as ye have been taught, abounding therein with thanksgiving" (Colossians 2:6-7). As we walk with the Lord, we grow closer to Him in spirit and faith. Our journey on earth becomes a closer walk with Him. Are you allowing your relationship with the Lord to mature?

August 20

"Forbearing one another, and forgiving one another, if any man have a quarrel against any: even as Christ forgave you, so also do ye" (Colossians 3:13). Jesus forgives us our trespasses and expects us to forgive each other also. If you are holding anger against someone, find a way to let it go. Ask Jesus for help in forgiving others. It is important to your own relationship with Him not to harbor ill will towards others. Do you have someone you need to forgive? Ask Jesus to help you.

August 21

In Paul's letter to the Thessalonians, he requested "Brethren, pray for us" (1 Thessalonians 5:25). The power of prayer is outstanding. Praying for each other is a wonderful gift to give. Prayers for healing, or understanding, for help with relationships or problems; prayers for any situations that cause concern. Of course, God already knows the situation, but our prayers show our love and concern for others, and express our free will to commune with the Lord. What concerns do you need to take to the Lord today?

August 22

"Praise ye the Lord. I will praise the Lord with my whole heart, in the assembly of the upright, and in the congregation" (Psalm 111:1). Praise Him through your art, through song, music, writing, your work with less fortunate people, or through whatever talents you have. We can each praise the Lord through developing our God-given talents and through using them to do the Lord's work. And giving Him the praise! What talent would you like to develop to work for the Lord?

August 23

"See that none render evil for evil unto any man; but ever follow that which is good, both among yourselves, and to all men" (1 Thessalonians 5:15). I can still hear my brothers' voices saying, "But he started it!" And Mom replying, "Well, you need to end it." When someone does a wrong or evil act toward you, it is tempting to hit them back. The Bible tells us to "end it" and not to allow the evil to continue. Blessed are the peacemakers... Have you ever taken on the role of peacemaker? How might you do so?

August 24

"For thou, Lord, art good, and ready to forgive; and plenteous in mercy unto all them that call upon thee" (Psalm 86:5). Many are the times that we stumble and fall, and just as many times God forgives us when we repent. The more we call upon Him for strength, the less often we will stumble and fall. Nourish your faith and strengthen your relationship with the Lord. What do you need to ask for God's help with today?

August 25

"I will remember the works of the Lord: surely I will remember thy wonders of old. I will meditate also of all thy work, and talk of thy doings" (Psalm 77:11-12). Reading the Bible helps us remember the awesome power of God. For example, the many miracles while leading the Israelites out of bondage in Egypt. Parting the Red Sea, feeding them Manna in the desert, bringing forth water from a rock. He can do all this and more, He can do wonders in your life also. What do you need help with today?

August 26

"Unto thee, O God, do we give thanks, *unto thee* do we give thanks: for that thy name is near thy wondrous works declare" (Psalm 75:1). The sunrise and sunsets declare the works of the Lord to us every day. Let us stop and see them anew and give thanks to the Lord. What other glorious sights do you see that bring words of thanks to your lips today? "O Lord our Lord, how excellent is thy name in all the earth! who has set thy glory above the heavens" (Psalm 8:1).

August 27

"Make a joyful noise unto God, all ye lands: Sing forth the honour of his name: make his praise glorious" (Psalm 66:1-2). Worship services often include music. For me, that is a wonderful way to worship and praise the Lord. My spirits soar with the swelling music and the people singing together warms my heart. I think that Jesus must enjoy hearing His people sing most of all. What is your favorite hymn? Sing it right now!

August 28

"Let us therefore come boldly unto the throne of grace, that we may obtain mercy, and find grace to help in time of need" (Hebrews 4:16). I can have confidence in the Lord, even when I do not have confidence in myself. I know that God will be with me and help me face whatever comes my way. "The righteous shall be glad in the Lord, and shall trust in him; and all the upright in heart shall glory" (Psalm 64:10). What are you facing that God can help you with today?

August 29

"In every thing give thanks: for this is the will of God in Christ Jesus concerning you" (1 Thessalonians 5:18). When we concentrate on what we have to be thankful for, we are less apt to become bogged down in negative thoughts. We are also making ourselves more aware of all that is good in our lives and all that is important. The more you give thanks, the more you will have to be thankful for. Nourish your relationship with God through thankful prayer. What are you thankful for today?

August 30

"Confess your faults to one another, and pray one for another, that ye may be healed. The effectual fervent prayer of a righteous man availeth much" (James 5:16). Jesus wants us to pray for each other. He already knows when someone needs something, but praying helps us to develop and express our compassion for others. Sometimes lifting others up to Jesus makes us realize our own needs and strengths as well. Who would you pray for today?

August 31

"For I the Lord thy God will hold thy right hand, saying unto thee, Fear not; I will help thee" (Isaiah 41:13). When we are fearful or worried, we have only to remember that God is near. Ask for His help through your prayers. Pour out your thoughts and feelings to Him and lift up your problems to Him. Place yourself in His able hands. He will help you through. Do you have worries that you need to pray about today?

September 1

The joy and peace that comes from knowing the love of Jesus is overwhelming. It spills into every aspect of life. It strengthens us for our everyday challenges and carries us through times of trouble. I want my family, friends, loved ones and indeed everyone on earth to know the love of Jesus. "Glory ye in his holy name: let the heart of them rejoice that seek the Lord" (Psalm 105:3). Who would you share God's love with today?

September 2

"O Lord, thou art my God; I will exalt thee, I will praise thy name; for thou hast done wonderful things; thy counsels of old are faithfulness and truth" (Isaiah 25:1). God is with us always. We may cloud our own vision and not be able to see that at times, but He is there when we open our hearts and pray. Is there anything you are having trouble understanding that you need to pray about today?

September 3

In his letter to the Corinthians, Paul said, "Know ye not that ye are the temple of God, and that the Spirit of God dwelleth in you?" (1 Corinthians 3:16). Beauty that comes from within is the lasting beauty of God's love shining through and showing on your face. There are many different body types and features. The important factor in beauty is the Spirit of God dwelling in you. Who would you like to share the beauty of God's love with today?

September 4

"My brethren, count it all joy when ye fall into divers temptations; Knowing this, that the trying of your faith worketh patience" (James 1:2-3). Practicing patience improves your capacity for patience. And practicing faith improves your faith. When we are severely tested, we come out stronger in the end. Strengthen your faith in the quiet times so you will be ready for the trying times. What do you need to practice patience with today? How will you go about it? Ask Jesus for His help.

September 5

"My lips shall greatly rejoice when I sing unto thee; and my soul, which thou hast redeemed" (Psalm 71:23). We rejoice when we think of the precious gift of His Son that God gave to us and of Jesus' gift to us of His life. It is hard to comprehend that depth of love. And to think, it is *given* to us. It is humbling and awe inspiring. Have you said a prayer of thanksgiving today? Go about your day greatly rejoicing!

September 6

"He hath made his wonderful works to be remembered: the Lord is gracious and full of compassion" (Psalm 111:4). How marvelous for us that God has compassion. We do try His patience and stand in need of His compassion. What are some things you do that God may not be pleased with? How can you change this into something that will please the Lord? "For the Lord taketh pleasure in his people: he will beautify the meek with salvation" (Psalm 149:4).

September 7

"Make me to go in the path of thy commandments; for therein do I delight" (Psalm 119:35). We want to follow Jesus and we don't have to do it alone. We can ask Him to help us. Knowing that we will weaken at times, we can ask Him for His strength. Shore up your faith every day and it will be there when you need it. Be prepared. Have you asked Jesus for His help in following His commandments?

September 8

"My hands also will I lift up unto thy commandments, which I have loved; and I will meditate in thy statutes" (Psalm 119:48). Thinking about the Word of God in the Bible helps us stay centered in faith. Lifting up our hands means doing something about the Word. Such as physically helping where we see a need. Maybe pitching in for work that needs to be done in your church. Or helping to clean up a playground in your community. What work can your hands do for the Lord?

September 9

"Thy hands have made me and fashioned me: give me understanding, that I may learn thy commandments" (Psalm 119:73). It isn't enough just to memorize God's commandments, we need to understand them and put them into practice. We study the Bible and pray for understanding. Love the Lord thy God with all thy heart and thy neighbor as thyself. How do you put this into practice in your life?

September 10

"Praise ye the Lord. Praise ye the Lord from the heavens: praise him in the heights. Praise ye him, all his angels: praise ye him, all his hosts" (Psalm 148:1-2). Imagine the glorious sound of angels singing God's praises. More beautiful than we can know. Yet, some day we hope to hear it, through God's grace and mercy. What blessings do you praise God for today?

September 11

On this day we remember the tragic events of 9/11. We honor the brave men and women who responded to assist and were harmed or killed during the aftermath. We mourn with those who lost loved ones and ask that Jesus' love surround them. "Blessed are they that mourn: for they shall be comforted" (Matthew 5:4). As a nation, we turn to God for healing and we pray for Him to guide us. What else do you need God's guidance about today?

September 12

"Wherefore comfort yourselves together, and edify one another, even as also ye do" (1 Thessalonians 5:11). Are there people in your life that you take for granted that they will always be there for you? Maybe parents, brother or sister, other relatives, a teacher or co-worker? The very ones we take for granted may be the most important people in our lives. Their dependability may be the very reason they are not often noticed or acknowledged. Take time to thank God for them. Take time to let them know how much they matter to you. No one is guaranteed tomorrow. You might just make their day.

September 13

"Thou art my portion, O Lord: I have said that I would keep thy words" (Psalm 119:57). It is good to remind ourselves that we serve the Lord. We have taken that stand and we walk in faith in God. All glory and honor be for the name of Jesus. Go forth and preach His gospel to all people. Who might you share His Word with today?

September 14

"Lay not up for yourselves treasures upon earth, where moth and rust doth corrupt, and where thieves break through and steal: But lay up for yourselves treasures in heaven, where neither moth nor rust doth corrupt, and where thieves do not break through nor steal: For where your treasure is, there will your heart be also" (Matthew 6:19-21). Take care that <u>you</u> own your possessions and they do not own you. Material things are not as important as people. Keep a healthy perspective about your things, your money, house, car, whatever else you have. God has commanded us to have no other gods before Him. Make sure your possessions do not become more important to you than God. Do you show God that He is more important to you than your possessions?

September 15

"Our help is in the name of the Lord, who made heaven and earth" (Psalm 124:8). However large our problems loom before us, we can know that God is able to help us. Having made the heavens and earth, He can certainly help us manage anything. Call upon His strength and wisdom and follow His path before you. He can guide you through anything, even if it seems to you to be too much to overcome. Take comfort in His strength. What problems do you need help with today?

September 16

"Let us not be desirous of vain glory, provoking one another, envying one another" (Galatians 5:26). How do you handle envy?

It is an emotion that crops up for most of us at one time or another. "I want that for myself" is often the first response. But the Bible tells us not to covet that which belongs to someone else. 'I am happy that my friend has that, and I hope to have one myself someday' is a more Christian attitude. We can learn to shape our reactions into healthy patterns. Jesus wants us to be happy, but not at someone else's expense. When we follow the commandment to love one another, we are happy for someone else's success even if we have not had that same success for ourselves yet. If you find resentment or envy creeping into your consciousness, rephrase the thoughts into something Jesus would agree with. Pray for Jesus' help to be able to have a Christian attitude. Think of the last time you were envious of someone. How might you have handled that better?

September 17

"Ponder the path of thy feet, and let all thy ways be established" (Proverbs 4:26). Do you ever get into trouble from jumping to conclusions? Think things over and make informed decisions. Be sure you have the facts correctly before making up your mind. When you establish yourself in faith, truth and integrity, your path becomes clearer. Pray for God to guide you in the path He would have you follow.

September 18

"Pleasant words are as an honeycomb, sweet to the soul, and health to the bones" (Proverbs 16:24). When we have God's love in our hearts and the peace of Christ in our lives, pleasant words are apt to be on our lips as well. A joyful attitude is apparent to those around you. Share God's love and you may help to draw others to Him. Who would you like to share God's love with today?

September 19

"Every man as he purposeth in his heart, so let him give; not grudgingly, or of necessity: for God loveth a cheerful giver" (2 Corinthians 9:7). Giving with a cheerful heart is a double blessing.

It fills you with joy and it causes joy for the receiver. Give of your time, your talents, your money or your skills – wherever you see the need. What might you do to help others today?

September 20

"And ye shall seek me, and find me, when ye shall search for me with all your heart" (Jeremiah 29:13). God is near, we just need to reach out and accept His love. Repent of our sins and ask for His grace and mercy. Invite Jesus into your heart and life. Share His love with those around you. Who would you like to share His love with today?

September 21

"Be of good courage, and he shall strengthen your heart, all ye that hope in the Lord" (Psalm 31:24). The road ahead of you may seem too hard to travel at times. Trust in the Lord and ask Him for the courage to continue. One step at a time, with the help of the Lord, all things are manageable. Trust Him. What problems do you face today? Have you lifted them to the Lord in prayer?

September 22

Thus will I bless thee while I live: I will lift up my hands in thy name" (Psalm 63:4). How do you lift up your hands to the Lord? Doing physical work for others is one way. Helping out with chores that need to be done in your church, such as yardwork is one example. Wherever your talents lie, that is where you can help. Taking groceries to someone who can't get out for themselves, or reading to the elderly may help. Where in your neighborhood can you lift up your hands in Jesus' name?

September 23

"The voice of the Lord is powerful; the voice of the Lord is full of majesty" (Psalm 29:4). God is great. Praise the Lord! We praise His name in all that we do and in all that we are. Lift up your voice and sing His praise. Let His love surround you and bask in the warmth of His loving arms. What blessings do you praise the Lord for today?

September 24

"For with thee is the fountain of life: in thy light shall we see light" (Psalm 36:9). Jesus is the light of the world. Cling to Him for hope, strength, and a light to your path. Without Him we do not see clearly, and we stumble on our way. Ask for His help to walk the straight and narrow, and He will be by your side. Have you asked Jesus' help with your path? Ask Him today.

September 25

"How excellent is thy lovingkindness, O God! therefore the children of men put their trust under the shadow of thy wings" (Psalm 36:7). Put your trust in Jesus. There is no safer place to be. He will comfort us through our hardships and lead us on the path to His peace. We do not have to go it alone – He is there for us. Call upon the Lord Jesus Christ, your Savior. What hardships do you need His help with today?

September 26

"Wait on the Lord: be of good courage, and he shall strengthen thine heart: wait, I say, on the Lord" (Psalm 27:14). We need to pray without ceasing and we also need to remember that things will happen in God's time schedule, not our own. Don't rush ahead, enjoy the here and now, and place your trust in God. Is there anything that you are impatient with that you need God's help to know His will?

September 27

"How much better is it to get wisdom than gold! and to get understanding rather to be chosen than silver" (Proverbs 16:16). We seek wisdom and understanding through prayer and Bible study. Knowing answers is important but knowing where to get the answers is the key. The answers are in the Good Book and prayer. What do you need God's help in understanding today?

September 28

"Commit thy works unto the Lord, and thy thoughts shall be established" (Proverbs chapter 16:3). Whatever point you are at in your life, you can commit your life to Jesus. Then whatever work or study you are doing becomes work for Him. We don't all have to be formal preachers to spread His Word and His love. Witness for Jesus throughout your everyday life. Someone around you may need to hear His Word. How might you witness for the Lord in your daily life?

September 29

"Let your conversation be without covetousness; and be content with such things as ye have: for he hath said, I will never leave thee, nor forsake thee" (Hebrews 13:5). Jesus, our Lord and Savior, is with us. What else could we want? Put things into perspective and prioritize your faith to the number one spot. How might you strengthen your relationship with Jesus?

September 30

A blessing given by Paul to the Corinthians: "Grace be unto you, and peace, from God our Father, and from the Lord Jesus Christ" (1 Corinthians 1:3). May the Lord be with you as you travel through this day. May He lead you and protect you. May you keep ever close to Him and receive His blessings. What are you thankful for on this day?

October 1

"I waited patiently for the Lord; and he inclined unto me, and heard my cry" (Psalm 40:1). Sometimes the hard part is waiting patiently. When we take our concerns to the Lord in prayer, we need to remember to say, "Thy will be done, not mine." We may know what we think needs to happen, but we don't have the bigger picture as God does. What problems do you need God's help with today? Thy will be done, O Lord.

October 2

"If my people, which are called by my name, shall humble themselves, and pray, and seek my face, and turn from their wicked ways; then will I hear from heaven, and will forgive their sin, and will heal their land" (2 Chronicles 7:14). Vice President Michael Pence opened his Bible to this verse when he was sworn in at the inauguration in 2017. Pray that all of our leaders will be guided by God and that all the people will come together in support of each other and of the leaders as well. Do you let your government representatives know that you want them to act in a Christian manner? Write or email them about your opinions.

October 3

"And in that day shall ye say, Praise the Lord, call upon his name, declare his doings among the people, make mention that his name is exalted" (Isaiah 12:4). We need to praise the Lord out loud as well as in our thoughts and private prayers. In this way we can be a witness for the Lord and share our faith with others. You never know who is noticing your actions and may be drawn to the Lord through you. Take any chance you find to sing His praises. Where might you be able to praise the Lord out loud today?

October 4

"O continue thy lovingkindness unto them that know thee; and thy righteousness to the upright in heart" (Psalm 36:10). When you know the love of God, you can't help but want others to know His love too. Spread the joy, spread His Word. Can you think of any place in your community where you could share God's love? Nursing homes are good places to bring some joy. Take a few friends and go help out at lunchtime, or see what else they may need that could use your help.

October 5

"But the salvation of the righteous is of the Lord: he is their strength in time of trouble" (Psalm 37:39). You do not have to solve your problems all by yourself. The Lord is with you. Draw strength from Him. Lift your problems to the Lord and lean on Him. You are not alone. God is able. What problems do you need God's strength for today?

October 6

"Peace I leave with you, my peace I give unto you: not as the world giveth, give I unto you. Let not your heart be troubled, neither let it be afraid" (John 14:27). Jesus offers us His peace. What a precious gift. Quiet your heart and hear His voice. Give thanks for having Him in your life. Seek His peace. Does anything trouble your heart today? Have you taken it to the Lord in prayer?

October 7

The Bible tells us that Moses said to the Lord, "Now therefore, I pray thee, if I have found grace in thy sight, shew me now thy way, that I may know thee, that I may find grace in thy sight" (Exodus 33:13 in part). Let us seek to find grace in the sight of the Lord. Study His commandments and make them the basis for living your life. In all things, seek His will. Do you live to find grace in His sight?

October 8

"The Lord will give strength unto his people; the Lord will bless his people with peace" (Psalm 29:11). What do you need help with from the Lord today? A prayer: O Lord, we ask that You strengthen us to be able to manage what we are facing day by day. Protect our loved ones and lead us to Your peace. Thy will be done, not ours. In Jesus' name. Amen.

October 9

"In the day of my trouble, I will call upon thee: for thou wilt answer me" (Psalm 86:7). Never hesitate to go to the Lord in prayer. Whatever you have gotten yourself into, He can help. Whether it is your own doing, or not, Jesus will be there for you. Don't let sinful pride, or embarrassment keep you from asking for help. Even when we do not deserve it, Jesus is still there for us and has compassion for us. Hallelujah for that good news! What do you need His help with today?

October 10

"The heavens declare the glory of God; and the firmament sheweth his handywork" (Psalm 19:1).
This world is so beautiful
And You gave it to us all.
The autumn colors, so fresh and bright
With crisp bright mornings and foggy nights.
Leaves falling, whirling all about
Children running, laughing – hear them shout!
Songs of praise we raise to Thee
For all the glorious sights we see.
The beauty that the sunset brings
We thank You, Lord, for all these things. Amen

What beauty in this world are you thankful to the Lord for providing to us?

October 11

"For the love of money is the root of all evil: which while some coveted after, they have erred from the faith, and pierced themselves through with many sorrows" (1 Timothy 6:10). It is necessary to earn money for most of us. We need to see that it keeps its proper place and does not become more important than God, faith, people, relationships or character in our lives. Do you have a healthy outlook toward money/wealth? Look into your heart and be sure you are not putting money ahead of the Lord.

October 12

"Sing unto the Lord, O ye saints of his, and give thanks at the remembrance of his holiness" (Psalm 30:4). With a thankful spirit we praise the name of Lord. Let us always be mindful of His presence in our lives. Always take thought for what He would have us to do. And support each other through the day, in His name and for His sake. Have you said a prayer of thankfulness today? Say one now.

October 13

"In thee, O Lord, do I put my trust; let me never be ashamed: deliver me in thy righteousness" (Psalm 31:1). Think upon that which is right and pray over what to do if you have questions. Keeping your faith strong will help you know God's will. Trust in Him for direction. Are there any questions that you are wrestling with today? Talk it over with the Lord.

October 14

"Rejoice in the Lord, O ye righteous: for praise is comely for the upright" (Psalm 33:1). Rejoice in the saving grace of the Lord. Praise His name in all your thoughts, words and deeds. Seek His comfort in times of sorrow and seek His guidance at all times. Grow your faith and your trust in Him. How do you praise the Lord in your actions? What else might you do to praise the Lord?

October 15

In this busy world where many demands are being made on our time, we need to set aside time each day to study the Word. Each time I read Bible passages, I learn something new from them. It may depend on my personal level of maturity and understanding at the time, or my needs of the moment; but even familiar verses often give me new meaning upon re-reading them. "For the word of the Lord is right; and all his works are done in truth" (Psalm

33:4). What is your favorite Bible verse? If you don't have one, pick one now!

October 16

"Our soul waiteth for the Lord: he is our help and our shield" (Psalm 33:20). Sometimes we have to wait to see what God has planned for us. This does not mean He has left our side. It may mean that we can't see clearly for all our anxiousness. It may mean that the time just has not come yet, for God's reasons. Whatever the circumstances, He is faithfully our help and shield. Trust in Him. Is there anything in your life that you are impatient about? Take it to the Lord in prayer.

October 17

"For our heart shall rejoice in him, because we have trusted in his holy name" (Psalm 33:21). Trust Him to lead you in the path that will fulfill the purpose He has for your life. Sometimes we know at least part of the purpose, for instance if you have been called to a profession, such as Pastor, nurse, teacher, etc. Sometimes we do not comprehend the purpose, but it is sufficient to know that God does, so we trust Him and go forward in His name. Have you let God know through your prayers that you want to follow Him?

October 18

"Let thy mercy, O Lord, be upon us, according as we hope in thee" (Psalm 33:22). We pray for that greatest of gifts – the grace and mercy of the Lord. We humbly ask for His grace and mercy as we strive to do His will here on earth. Knowing that we are not perfect, we strive to do our best, improve with His help, and listen always for His will. Thanks be to God. What are some things that God wants us all to do? Do you do those things?

October 19

"O magnify the Lord with me, and let us exalt his name together" (Psalm 34:3). Worshiping God in the presence of other people is very uplifting. Our songs do seem magnified when many voices are combined. I can imagine that this is pleasing to the Lord, so what better reason to do it. We are all God's children and none of us are perfect. We should not expect perfection from our fellow church goers, but rather support each other as much as we can and pray for each other. Who do you know that might need your prayers for support? Pray for them.

October 20

In his letter to the Thessalonians, Paul said "We give thanks to God always for you all, making mention of you in our prayers" (1 Thessalonians 1:2). Let us also remember our loved ones in our prayers. As we ask God for His blessings upon them, we also remind ourselves of their importance in our lives. Remember also to let them know they are loved – make their day! Who would you ask God to bless today?

October 21

"The day is thine, the night also is thine: thou hast prepared the light and the sun. Thou hast set all the borders of the earth: thou hast made summer and winter" (Psalm 74:16-17). Everything belongs to the Lord. He has given us the job of caretaker for the earth. We see His beauty surrounding us every day. We should be good stewards for the earth and for each other. Take care to tend to your corner of the world and those in it. What might you do to care for the earth?

October 22

"For the Lord God is a sun and a shield: the Lord will give grace and glory: no good thing will he withhold from them that walk uprightly" (Psalm 84:11). Jesus is our rock, our shelter and shield. Come to Him with all your cares. All things are possible in Him. Praise God! What cares do you have to share with the Lord in prayer?

October 23

"O Lord of hosts, blessed is the man that trusteth in thee" (Psalm 84:12). Trust in the Lord and abide by His commandments. Our journey through life will be full of ups and downs. We need His help to navigate our path. Let us follow His rules and follow His will. Then we will know we are on the right path. Do you follow His will and ask for His help in your daily life?

October 24

This is Paul speaking about God in his letter to the Ephesians. "Now to him that is able to do exceedingly abundantly above all that we ask or think, according to the power that worketh in us, Unto him be glory in the church by Christ Jesus throughout all ages, world without end. Amen" (Ephesians 3:20-21). As we go out into the world, let us remember to take our faith with us through the day. The things that we do during the day can be done to the glory of the Lord. As we give Him credit for what He has enabled us to do, we show our faith to others. The light of His love shows through in our actions when we work to His glory. What might you do this day that shows your faith to others?

October 25

"Wherefore putting away lying, speak every man truth with his neighbour: for we are members one of another" (Ephesians 4:25). Our actions affect more than just ourselves. We are members of many different groups of people. We need to deal honestly within all our groups. "Thou shalt not bear false witness" (Exodus 20:16) applies in all situations. Are you honest in your dealings with others and with yourself?

October 26

"Be ye therefore followers of God, as dear children; And walk in love, as Christ also hath loved us" (Ephesians 5:1-2 in part). Jesus spoke His message of love and also lived His message of love. He told us to love one another and He also showed us what that meant.

He spoke with everyone, He took care of the poor and needy, healed the sick, and loved us all enough to die for us. We can do His work by helping wherever we are able. What can you think of to help those less fortunate than you?

October 27

Paul wrote these words to the Corinthians: "God is faithful, by whom ye were called unto the fellowship of his Son Jesus Christ our Lord" (1 Corinthians 1:9). Being called to a Christian life is a miraculous gift. We can all do His work with whatever talents He has given us. Let us look around at our corner of the world and see what we can do to bring Jesus' love to others who may not know Him. What talents or skills would you like to develop? How might you use them to share God's Word?

October 28

"Therefore thou shalt love the Lord thy God, and keep his charge, and his statutes, and his judgements, and his commandments, always" (Deuteronomy 11:1). As we read and study the Bible, we pray for understanding of God's commandments and how they fit into our everyday lives. We pray for God to guide us in His path of righteousness. We look for God's mercy and His peace. Does your daily life show that you follow Jesus? What more might you do to show your love for the Lord?

October 29

"He hath shewed thee, O man, what is good; and what doth the Lord require of thee, but to do justly, and to love mercy, and to walk humbly with thy God: (Micah 6:8). Let us try to act with justice toward others, to show mercy to everyone and to walk humbly, as the Lord would have us do. Sometimes we find humility hard to practice as we think we know what is best. If we find ourselves telling the Lord what we need, we may want to turn that around and ask Him what He wants us to do. Do you have concerns in your life that you need help with? Have you taken them to the Lord in prayer?

October 30

"I will be glad and rejoice in thy mercy: for thou hast considered my trouble; thou hast known my soul in adversities" (Psalm 31:7). Jesus knows who and what we are, and He loves us. Accept His love and know that you did not have to earn it, you only have to embrace it. Because we love Jesus, we do try to be good people and do His will. But Jesus does not withhold His love until you become a better person. Give your anxieties to Him and replace them with His love. What worries do you need to lift to the Lord in prayer today?

October 31

"The Lord is gracious, and full of compassion; slow to anger, and of great mercy" (Psalm 145:8). As we follow Jesus we need to take care to also show compassion to others, and to be slow to anger. Where in your life have you seen the need for compassion and mercy for someone else? A prayer: Lord, we are thankful for Your grace and mercy. We ask forgiveness for our sins and pray You would help us to do Your will. Be ever near to us. Bless and keep our loved ones. In Jesus' name and for His sake. Amen.

November 1

"I exhort therefore, that, first of all, supplications, prayers, intercessions, and giving of thanks, be made for all men; For kings, and for all that are in authority; that we may lead a quiet and peaceable life in all godliness and honesty" (1 Timothy 2:1-2). Pray for our government leaders, that they might listen for God's advice and ask Him to guide them in making decisions. We all need to do our part as individuals and our elected officials have an even greater responsibility as they end up speaking for everyone. In turn, we need to let our elected officials know how we feel and what we think about issues that affect us all so that they will better represent us. We need to ask God what His will is and listen to His answer. "Thy will be done" should be our fervent prayer. What are some issues currently facing our government officials? How might you decide the issues if you were in charge? Write or email your representatives.

November 2

"Serve the Lord with gladness: come before his presence with singing" (Psalm 100:2). When I was a child, a preacher and his family were invited to our church for a revival. We had a wonderful week of music, singing, preaching and witnessing for Jesus. It was a truly inspiring time. I remember being particularly impressed with how happy and full of joy this preacher's children were. They taught me that while there is a time for quiet pious worship, there is also a time for making a joyful noise unto the Lord. What joy do you have in your heart today? Share it with the Lord in prayer.

November 3

Hardships and problems often bring us life lessons. Either as they are occurring, or in hindsight. How we handle problems can show a lot about ourselves. Most important is to learn the lesson so that we don't repeat the problem (especially if it is one of our own making). If you have developed the habit of leaning on the Lord, your automatic reaction to hardships will be prayer. "Many are the afflictions of the righteous: but the Lord delivereth him out of them all" (Psalm 34:19). What problems are you facing? Be faithful to lift them in prayer.

November 4

"And he commanded the multitude to sit down on the grass, and took the five loaves, and the two fishes, and looking up to heaven, he blessed, and brake, and gave the loaves to his disciples, and the disciples to the multitude. And they did all eat, and were filled: and they took up of the fragments that remained twelve baskets full" (Matthew 14:19-20). What little we have to give to Jesus, He can multiply into a surplus. This reminds us not to hold back from doing a good work simply because we may feel it is too little to really help. You never know how Jesus will multiply your small offering. What do you have to offer as a good work for the Lord?

November 5

"I will praise the name of God with a song, and will magnify him with thanksgiving" (Psalm 69:30). With a song in your heart and His praise on your lips, you can worship the Lord wherever you are. We don't have to wait for Sunday morning to sing God's praises. Pop some gospel tunes on your radio and sing along! What is your favorite hymn? What words in the song do you like best?

November 6

"Let no corrupt communication proceed out of your mouth, but that which is good to the use of edifying, that it may minister grace unto the hearers" (Ephesians 4:29). We need to deal honestly with others and with ourselves as well. Jesus commanded us to love our neighbors as ourselves. So, we need to be honest and respectful in all our dealings. Gossip, disrespect, or bullying is not consistent with Christian values. What can you do if you see these things taking place in your school or workplace?

November 7

This was Paul's prayer for the Ephesians many years ago: "That Christ may dwell in your hearts by faith; that ye, being rooted and grounded in love, May be able to comprehend with all saints what is the breadth, and length, and depth, and height; And to know the love of Christ, which passeth knowledge, that ye might be filled with all the fullness of God" (Ephesians 3:17- 19). This is my prayer for us all today. What do you need to pray about this day?

November 8

"My soul, wait thou only upon God; for my expectation is from him. He only is my rock and my salvation: he is my defence; I shall not be moved" (Psalm 62:5-6). Do you sometimes find that you are putting roadblocks into your own way? Listing out all the reason that you can't do something, for instance. Instead of thinking about the ways it can be done. Pray about the situation and lift it up to the Lord. Ask for His will to be done.

November 9

"Hear my voice, O God, in my prayer: preserve my life from fear of the enemy" (Psalm 64:1). Unfortunately, there is evil in this world. We need to stay close to God to keep away from evil. And we need His help in dealing with evil wherever we find it. What do you see as evil going on around you? Have you prayed for God's help to deal with it? Lift it to the Lord in prayer.

November 10

"All the earth shall worship thee, and shall sing unto thee; they shall sing to thy name" (Psalm 66:4 in part). This will be a glorious day indeed when all the earth sings God's praise. Do your part to spread His Word. Sing His praises at every opportunity. Others may be drawn to Jesus through your witness, through seeing how you live your life for the Lord. How do you show that you follow Jesus? What else might you do in your daily life to witness for the Lord?

November 11

On this Veteran's Day we take the time to thank all our awesome veterans for their service to our country. We ask God to bless those who have served and those who are presently in service. Let us also pray for their family members who have sacrificed as well. Jesus Himself said, "Greater love hath no man than this, that a man lay down his life for his friends" (John 15:13). Let us recognize that those who lived through military service often have much burden to bear and support them however we can. How might you let a veteran know that their service is appreciated?

November 12

"But verily God hath heard me; he hath attended to the voice of my prayer. Blessed be God, which hath not turned away my prayer, nor his mercy from me" (Psalm 66:19-20). Let us remember to say, "Thank You" to God as often as we have said "Please." Sometimes we sort of run away in our happiness with answered prayer and forget to say how thankful we are. Even if you have not seen the answer yet, remember to say, "Thank You" for listening, and to pray "Thy will be done." What prayers has God answered for you?

November 13

"Keep yourselves in the love of God, looking for the mercy of our Lord Jesus Christ unto eternal life. And of some have compassion making a difference" (Jude 1:21-22). Pray on all things. Make a difference in someone else's life wherever you can. Look to God for your inspiration and salvation. How might you make a difference in someone else's life?

November 14

"I am Alpha and Omega, the beginning and the ending, saith the Lord, which is, and which was, and which is to come, the Almighty" (Revelations 1:8). God is with us, has always been with us, and will always be with us. We can take comfort that He is near. When we repent of our sins and follow Him, we are protected by His love. He will help us through whatever problems the world has around us. What problems are you facing now? Call on Him.

November 15

"Jesus answered and said unto him, If a man love me, he will keep my words: and my Father will love him, and we will come unto him, and make our abode with him" (John 14:23). We show our love for Jesus by keeping His commandments to love the Lord with all our heart, soul, and mind, and to love our neighbors as ourselves. How do you show that you love your neighbors? What else might you be able to do?

November 16

"As the Father hath loved me, so have I loved you: continue ye in my love" (John 15:9). Jesus prepares the disciples for His leaving them, and lets them know that His love will not leave them. We also can be confident in His love. Keep Him near to you through prayer. How do you let Jesus know that you love Him? What else might you do?

November 17

"But I will hope continually, and will yet praise thee more and more. My mouth shall shew forth thy righteousness and thy salvation all the day" (Psalm 71:14-15 in part). Our hope comes from God. We praise His name for the blessings He has given us in our lives. Pass along God's love and peace through helping out other people around you and in your community, in His name. Where do you see a need that you might help fill?

November 18

"Help us, O God of our salvation, for the glory of thy name: and deliver us, and purge away our sins, for thy name's sake" (Psalm 79:9). A prayer: Forgive us, O Lord, for our sins of the past and help us not to repeat them. Keep us on the path of Your will for our lives. Grant us strength to follow You. Thank You for all You have done for us. Amen. Are there things in your life that you need to let go of and not repeat? Ask for God's help.

November 19

"O sing unto the Lord a new song: sing unto the Lord, all the earth. Sing unto the Lord, bless his name; shew forth his salvation from day to day" (Psalm 96:1-2). Living day to day and showing that we are Christians by our way of dealing with other people is a challenge. Prayer and praise helps us maintain the right attitude. What struggles do you have with daily life? Are you faithful to take them to the Lord in prayer?

November 20

"Sing unto the Lord; for he hath done excellent things: this is known in all the earth" (Isaiah 12:5). I am thankful to God for all the excellent things He has done for me and my family. Most of all for giving His Son Jesus to die for our sins. I am thankful for all the answered prayer for healing that He has granted us. And for all the times He has seen us through troubles. What are you thankful for? Take a minute to think it through and then offer your prayers of thanksgiving.

November 21

"Withhold not good from them to whom it is due, when it is in the power of thine hand to do it" (Proverbs 3:27). Helping others can take many forms. Giving money or food to a food bank; helping out in the kitchens of homeless shelters; organizing a clothing drive or similar charity; these are all ways of sharing God's love. Singing to nursing home residents if that is your talent, or reading to those who don't see well anymore are also ways to share. What other ways can you think of to share God's love?

November 22

"…in everything by prayer and supplication with thanksgiving let your requests be made known unto God. And the peace of God, which passeth all understanding, shall keep your hearts and minds through Jesus Christ" (Philippians 4:6-7 in part). Thanksgiving season is uplifting and joyful as we remember all the blessings we have been given. Let us also remember to share our bounty with others less fortunate, in order to pass along those blessings. What would you like to share? How might you do that?

November 23

"O give thanks unto the Lord; for he is good: for his mercy endureth for ever" (Psalm 136:1). I am thankful for faith, family, friends, and health. Focusing on the blessings in life brings peace of mind and makes it easier to put the problems into perspective. What blessings are you thankful for this Thanksgiving season? Share each one with the Lord in prayer.

November 24

"Finally, brethren, whatsoever things are true, whatsoever things are honest, whatsoever things are just, whatsoever things are pure, whatsoever things are lovely, whatsoever things are of good report; if there be any virtue, and if there be any praise, think on these things" (Philippians 4:8). Give thanks for all the good things in the world and do your part to increase them. Put away negativity and promote the positive in your life. What things do you need to let go of? Have you asked God to help you?

November 25

"Let brotherly love continue. Be not forgetful to entertain strangers; for thereby some have entertained angels unawares" (Hebrews 13:1-2). Helping others less fortunate than ourselves should be a year-round activity. We especially remember to support food banks and homeless shelters around Thanksgiving. Let us continue this support throughout the year and be aware that you may be entertaining angels! What might you do to help others?

November 26

"It is a good thing to give thanks unto the Lord, and to sing praises unto thy name, O most High: To shew forth thy lovingkindness in the morning and thy faithfulness every night" (Psalm 92:1-2). We are ever grateful for God's grace and mercy – without which none of us would be saved. We are so blessed that God is mindful of us. What are you thankful for in your life?

November 27

"Let, I pray thee, thy merciful kindness be for my comfort, according to thy word unto thy servant" (Psalm 119:76). If you are feeling sad or lonesome during the holidays, share your feelings with God in prayer. Talk over your situation and ask God's help with your path. Seeking company might lift your spirits too. Volunteer at a homeless shelter or seek out a church service. What other ways might you connect or reconnect with your community?

November 28

"Blessed are the peacemakers: for they shall be called the children of God" (Matthew 5:9). Jesus wants us to live in peace with each other. If we follow His example of brotherly love, the world would be a more peaceful place. Let us try to resolve conflict wherever we find it, instead of turning conflict into hate. Do you have any areas in your life that are not peaceful? What might you do to encourage peace?

November 29

"Lay not up for yourselves treasures upon earth, where moth and rust doth corrupt, and where thieves break through and steal. But lay up for yourselves treasures in heaven, where neither moth nor rust doth corrupt, and where thieves do not break through nor steal. For where your treasure is, there will your heart be also" (Matthew 6:19-21). These verses remind us to store up good deeds rather than material possessions. People are more important than things. Do you have the right outlook on people as compared to possessions?

November 30

"Be glad in the Lord, and rejoice, ye righteous: and shout for joy, all ye that are upright in heart" (Psalm 32:11). How often have you shouted for joy lately? When I see young children shout for joy I remember the feeling very well, but don't recall doing it for a long time. We need to relearn the simple joys of life and the simple responses that came so naturally as children. Shout for joy that Jesus loves you! Amen! What other reasons do you have to shout for joy?

December 1

Advent is the time leading up to Christmas. The traditional preparing for Christmas day happens during this time. The Advent season focuses on the fact that Christ came into the world, that He is present in the world today, and that He will return at the Second Coming. Love, joy and peace symbolize the expectation of the birth of Jesus. Take time to read Luke chapter 2 verses 1 through 20 which describe this awesome event. "For unto you is born this day in the city of David a Savior, which is Christ the Lord" (Luke 2:11). Are you prepared to receive His love, joy and peace?

December 2

"For as the rain cometh down, and the snow from heaven, and returneth not thither, but watereth the earth, and maketh it bring forth and bud, that it may give seed to the sower and bread to the eater" (Isaiah 55:10).
Snow is whirling all around
Gently blanketing the ground
White and pure as it floats on air
Thank You, Lord, for sending it there.
Settling around us like a rug
The snow gives us a heavenly hug.
Descending gently like a dove
Covering us, as does God's love.

What do you want to thank God for on this day?

December 3

The Bible tells us that when Joseph first heard that his fiancée, Mary, was with child, he planned to send her away quietly so as not to make her a public example, as he was a just man (in Matthew 1:18-19). But then an angel spoke to Joseph in a dream and told him the child was of God and was to be called Emmanuel, meaning "God with us." "Then Joseph being raised from sleep did as the angel of the Lord had bidden him" (Matthew 1:24). Have you ever almost thrown away an opportunity because of first reactions? Sometimes God is giving us opportunities that we do not recognize because of our pre-conceived notions. Think and pray before you act.

December 4

Can you imagine what Mary must have thought when the angel Gabriel told her that she would have a child and He would be the Son of God? Mary asked how that could be and the angel told her, "For with God nothing shall be impossible. And Mary said, Behold the handmaid of the Lord; be it unto me according to thy word. And the angel departed from her" (Luke 1:37-38). Mary did not try to get out of it or ask for assurances for herself or her safety. No excuses, no bargaining, just acceptance and obedience. Would you be able to do the same?

December 5

"Sing, O heavens; and be joyful, O earth; and break forth into singing, O mountains: for the Lord hath comforted his people, and will have mercy on his afflicted" (Isaiah 49:13). Being Christian does not mean that we will not have problems in life. But it does mean that we will not be on our own to solve those problems. We have Jesus' help and He is by our side. Call on Him through prayer. Have faith in Him to help you through. Surround yourself in His love and protection. What do you need to pray for right now?

December 6

"Praise ye the Lord. O give thanks unto the Lord; for he is good: for his mercy endureth for ever" (Psalm 106:1). Take time throughout your day to say, "Thank You, Lord" when you notice something for which you are thankful. Such as a beautiful sunrise or sunset, or family and friends. It could be the smile of a child, or much needed rain. Take the time to notice and say thank you – out loud, if you can. Developing this habit makes for a calmer, more pleasant day. And as often as it is appropriate to do so out loud, it is a small way to witness for the Lord. What are you thankful for today?

December 7

"If ye keep my commandments, ye shall abide in my love; even as I have kept my Father's commandments, and abide in his love" (John 15:10). Jesus tells us how to abide in His love. We are to keep His commandments to love the Lord our God and to love one another as He loved us. Examine your thoughts, words, and deeds and be sure you are keeping His commandments. Ask for His help along your journey. Are you keeping His commandments?

December 8

In Luke 12:15, Jesus tells us, "Take heed, and beware of covetousness: for a man's life consisteth not in the abundance of the things which he possesses." Let us take care that we do not value things above people. Also, that we do not become so intent on acquiring possessions that we ignore acquiring knowledge and faith. Feed your spiritual growth. How are you working toward gaining more knowledge of the Bible, and toward a closer walk with Jesus?

December 9

"And it shall come to pass, that whosoever shall call on the name of the Lord shall be saved" (Acts 2:21). Call on the Lord to help you through this day. What do you most need help with? What are you most thankful for? Keep Jesus close in your thoughts. Nurture your prayer life and calling upon God will become your first response in any situation.

December 10

"If we confess our sins, he is faithful and just to forgive us our sins, and to cleanse us from all unrighteousness" (1 John 1:9). We all make mistakes. Ask for forgiveness when you realize you have sinned. Learn, grow, and do not repeat those mistakes. God grants us His grace and mercy when we repent and ask for forgiveness. Is there anything in your life that you need to guard against repeating? Think about how to do this and ask for His help.

December 11

"Let love be without dissimulation. Abhor that which is evil; cleave to that which is good" (Romans 12:9). A prayer: O Lord, help us strive to be humble, honest, kind, faithful and helpful. Help us strive not to be hypocritical, dishonest, prideful, back-biting or bullying. Help us to live our lives in such a way as to reflect Your love to the world around us. Amen. What traits do you need to work on the most? How will you go about it?

December 12

"And this is his commandment, That we should believe on the name of his Son Jesus Christ, and love one another, as he gave us commandment" (1 John 3:23). Loving one another should include having respect for others and helping where we see a need, according to our own abilities. Sometimes all we can do is offer a listening ear, we can't always solve the problem. What does loving one another look like to you? How do you put this into practice?

December 13

"And he that keepeth his commandments dwelleth in him, and he in him. And hereby we know that he abideth in us, by the Spirit which he has given us" (1 John 3:24). As you live your life, would someone (who did not know you) be able to tell that you are a Christian? Look for those little opportunities during your day to witness for God. "Praise the Lord for that" or "I'll say a prayer for you" in your conversation is a small way to let others know of your faith. What other ways can you think of to show your faith?

December 14

Some people have sadness associated with holidays. Possibly because of a loved one passing away close to this date, or many other reasons. It can be difficult to share in the joy that others around you are showing if you are depressed or sad yourself. Talk to God in prayer and lift your burden up to Him. Spill out your feelings to the Lord and do not keep them bottled up. He understands. To those who do not have this sadness, be aware of anyone around you who does, and do what you can to help them deal with their feelings. "Humble yourselves therefore under the mighty hand of God, that he may exalt you in due time: Casting all your care upon him; for he careth for you" (1 Peter 5:6-7). Do you know anyone who might need your help right now? What might you be able to do for them?

December 15

"Herein is love, not that we loved God, but that he loved us, and sent his Son to be the propitiation for our sins. Beloved, if God so loved us, we ought also to love one another" (1 John 4:10-11). God's love is the greatest love you could think of. We are not worthy of it, but we receive it nevertheless. His grace and mercy are given to us when we repent of our sins and turn to Him. Hallelujah for this greatest of blessings! How might you share God's love with others?

December 16

"The Lord thy God in the midst of thee is mighty; he will save, he will rejoice over thee with joy; he will rest in his love, he will joy over thee with singing" (Zephaniah 3:17). Jesus tells us, in Luke 15:11-32, in the parable of the prodigal son that there is much joy when one who is lost returns to the fold. There are so many of us that it is hard to understand how Jesus can notice every one of us, yet He does. He said that the very hair of our heads is numbered (in Luke 12:7). Awesome and humbling. Have you said, "Thank You, Lord" today? Say a prayer of thanksgiving now.

December 17

"The Lord is my portion, saith my soul; therefore I will hope in him. The Lord is good unto them that wait for him, to the soul that seeketh him" (Lamentations 3:24-25). Attending worship services, daily prayer, Bible reading, Bible study and doing God's work are all ways to nourish your faith. Outreach and witnessing for God can take many forms, depending on your specific talents. What ways can you think of to do God's work in your community?

December 18

"Let the word of Christ dwell in you richly in all wisdom; teaching and admonishing one another in psalms and hymns and spiritual songs, singing with grace in your hearts to the Lord" (Colossians 3:16). Singing Christmas carols brings joy to those singing as well as those who hear them. Where could you take a group Christmas caroling and bring joy to someone's heart this Christmas? Nursing homes, mall corridors, or senior centers might be good places.

December 19

"Give ear to my words, O Lord, consider my meditation. Hearken unto the voice of my cry, my King, and my God: for unto thee will I pray" (Psalm 5:1-2). We pray for ourselves and each other when we see a need to do so, or hear of a problem that someone is having. Yes, God already knows of those problems, but saying our prayers helps us develop and express our own compassion as well as lifting the person up to the Lord. God gave us free will and we need to exercise it for one another's benefit. Who might you pray for today?

December 20

"In this was manifested the love of God toward us, because that God sent his only begotten Son into the world, that we might live through him" (1 John 4:9). As Christmas day approaches, take time to marvel at the greatest of gifts that God gave to us. Share His love with others around you. Pass along His peace wherever you can. Who would you like to share God's love with today? Merry Christmas!

December 21

"And she shall bring forth a son, and thou shalt call his name JESUS: for he shall save his people from their sins" (Matthew 1:21). God's gift to us of His Son at the first Christmas was truly the greatest gift of all. We give gifts to each other at Christmas time to share the joy and love of the first Christmas. Let us always remember the reason for the season. It is more about sharing love and less about which gift to give which person, or wondering what gift am I going to receive. Take time away from the hustle and bustle to quietly reflect on the joy of Christmas and give thanks. Have you said, "Thank You" to God for His greatest gift to you?

December 22

The Baby Jesus was poor in material possessions but rich beyond measure in love. The Bible tells us that Jesus said, "For ye have the poor always with you; but me ye have not always (Matthew 26:11)". Giving to others less fortunate than ourselves helps us show our love for Jesus. We can give in different ways (of our material possessions, of our time or of our talents) depending on what we have available. Gifts of love do not necessarily have to cost money. What ways might you give this Christmas?

December 23

Joy to the world! "And the angel said unto them, Fear not: for, behold, I bring you good tidings of great joy which shall be to all people" (Luke 2:10). The Savior is born, and *all* people may share this joy. This excellent news is the reason for the unbounded joy at Christmas time. It makes us more charitable to our friends as well as people we don't know. Hold on to this feeling all year – it is true on a daily basis, not just for the week of Christmas. With a smile on your face and a song in your heart, keep the spirit of Christmas year-round! Who would you like to share the joy of Christmas with today?

December 24

When the angel appeared to the shepherds to tell them the good news of Christ's birth, the Bible says, "And suddenly there was with the angel a multitude of the heavenly host praising God, and saying, Glory to God in the highest, and on earth peace, good will toward men" (Luke 2:13-14). What a glorious sound and marvelous sight this must have been. Our work now is to achieve goodwill with other people. How might you show good will to others today?

December 25

"And so it was, that, while they were there, the days were accomplished that she should be delivered. And she brought forth her firstborn son, and wrapped him in swaddling clothes, and laid him in a manger; because there was no room for them in the inn" (Luke 2:6-7). Jesus arrived as a newborn baby in quiet circumstances on earth, but the heavens declared His arrival in glory. The angles announced to the shepherds, "For unto you is born this day in the city of David a Saviour, which is Christ the Lord" (Luke 2:11). Hallelujah! Can you imagine the shepherds' amazement? We should be just as amazed today. What might you do to share that amazement with others?

December 26

What did you get for Christmas? I hope your first answer is a closer relationship with God. The material things that we get for Christmas are fleeting and not important in the grand scheme of life. The joy of renewing our faith and remembering that God sent His Son to be with us is the best Christmas present ever. God gave us the greatest of gifts. Rejoice in His presence! "Glory ye in his holy name: let the heart of them rejoice that seek the Lord" (1 Chronicles 16:10). Think again, -What did you get for Christmas?

December 27

"It is of the Lord's mercies that we are not consumed, because his compassions fail not. They are new every morning: great is thy faithfulness" (Lamentations 3:22-23). God's compassion embraces us all. For this, we give our most sincere thanks. His mercy and compassion are far greater than we can imagine. We need to remember not to take Him for granted, and to say our prayers of thankfulness and gratitude. A prayer: Thank You, Lord, for all that You do for us. Amen. What might you do to show your thankfulness for God's compassion?

December 28

"When they saw the star, they rejoiced with exceeding great joy. And when they were come into the house, they saw the young child with Mary his mother, and fell down and worshipped him: and when they had opened their treasures, they presented unto him gifts; gold, and frankincense, and myrrh" (Matthew 2:10-11). The wise men travelled far to see Jesus and brought Him precious gifts. Today we can kneel and pray and give Him gifts of our prayers, our time and our talents. What gifts would you give to Jesus?

December 29

Are you looking forward to the new year? As you think back over this year, do you have any goals that you lost track of, or anything you started but forgot to finish? Take some time to reflect on your relationship with God and note any progress that you have made. Note also any areas that you want to work on. Ask for God's help in keeping your thoughts and actions pleasing in His sight. "The steps of a good man are ordered by the Lord: and he delighteth in his way. Though he fall, he shall not be utterly cast down: for the Lord upholdeth him with his hand" (Psalm 37:23-24).

December 30

"But God commendeth his love toward us, in that, while we were yet sinners, Christ died for us" (Romans 5:8). As I was putting away my Christmas decorations, I was carefully wrapping my Nativity figures in tissue paper to protect them. It occurred to me that just as we protect our possessions, we need to protect ourselves. Protect your relationship with God by paying attention to it, putting time into it, and striving to understand His teachings to the best of your abilities. Reading the Bible, Bible study, daily devotions and prayers are some ways to go about this. What other ways can you think of to protect your relationship with God?

December 31

"Be ye strong therefore, and let not your hands be weak: for your work shall be rewarded" (2 Chronicles 15:7). Reflecting upon the past year helps us see where we have been and helps us know where we are headed. Making resolutions for the coming new year can help us get on course or stay on course for where we want to go. Achieving a closer relationship with God can happen in any number of ways. Just knowing that you want to be a good servant to the Lord is a good beginning. What goals do you have for the new year? What work could you do for the Lord?

ABOUT THE AUTHOR

Gwen McQuesten Keegan was born and raised in the small town of South Shore, Kentucky, and grew up within the loving arms of the Methodist Church. She moved to California at age 26 and has lived in several cities and towns there. Currently she lives in El Dorado Hills, California with her husband, Dennis who is a native of San Francisco. They visit Kentucky frequently and enjoy attending the same Methodist church of her childhood.

Made in the USA
San Bernardino, CA
11 July 2018